AMC guide to

COUNTRY WALKS NEAR BALTIMORE

within reach by
public transportation

by Alan Fisher

COUNTRY WALKS NEAR BALTIMORE
Copyright © 1981 by Alan Hall Fisher

Printed in the United States of America.
If you find any errors in the text or maps, or can suggest improvements, you are urged to send a letter to the Appalachian Mountain Club, attention Country Walks, 5 Joy Street, Boston, Massachusetts 02108.

FIRST EDITION

Edited by Arlyn Powell and Jeri Kane
Composition by Gayle Morrison
Cover photos by Steve Wilcoxson
Cover design by Betsey Tryon
Photos & maps by Alan Fisher
Production by Michael Cirone and Betsey Tryon
Printing & Binding by Heffernan Press
Cover Printing by John Pow Co.

ISBN 0-910146-36-5

CONTENTS

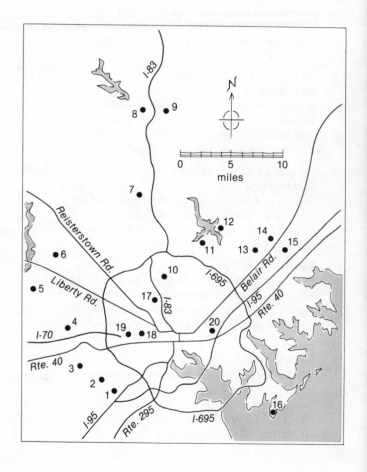

FOREWORD

THERE'S STILL TIME for a walk in the woods, even if you've spent all morning working or sleeping late.

This book is for people who want an outing in the country without wasting half the day getting there and coming back. If you live in the Baltimore area, the excursions described here are close at hand. Most are within reach of the city by bus; all are easily reached by car. The walks have been planned to show the best parts of Baltimore's countryside and to encourage everyone to use the many large parks and extensive trail networks maintained by state, county, and city agencies and private conservation groups.

Each chapter of this book includes directions, a map, and a commentary on the area's natural or social history or other

1

pertinent issues. The routes cover the gamut of Maryland's Piedmont and Coastal Plain landscapes: steep-sided river valleys, farmland, rolling hills, rocky barrens, floodplain, marsh, and shore, as well as historic houses, mill sites, and ruins along the way. All the areas included here are open to the public, and many are excellent for ski touring as well as walking. The excursions are attractive at all times of year, and successive visits at different seasons provide an added dimension of enjoyment due to the changing foliage, views, flowers, birds, and wildlife.

Although most of the routes described here are not rugged, a few precautions are in order. Wear shoes that you do not mind getting muddy or wet. Sneakers or thick-soled running shoes are adequate (except in cold weather); hiking shoes or boots are better. I usually carry a small knapsack containing a few sandwiches, a plastic water bottle, a sweater, a rain parka, and some insect repellent during summer and early fall. During the warmer months check your clothing and body for ticks when you return from your walk. In the relatively few instances where the routes follow roads for short distances, walk on the left shoulder facing the oncoming traffic. To help maintain the trails free from drooping branches, you may want to bring a small pair of shears. And remember when allotting time that two miles per hour is a typical walking pace for a leisurely excursion.

If you plan to take a bus of the Mass Transit Administration (MTA), always call 539-5000 beforehand to check on the route, schedule, and connecting buses for the trip both out and back. Specify the day that you are thinking of going; bus schedules and routes frequently are different for weekdays, Saturday, and Sunday.

About trash. Dumping is a problem that plagues our state and local parks. Some businesses appear to make regular use of the parks to dispose of their used tires, rubbish, construction rubble, or whatever. If you see someone dumping refuse, note the license number of his vehicle and report the incident to the agency that manages the park (listed in the introduction to each chapter). Also, urge the park agencies to construct and maintain effective barriers to prevent dumpers from driving into the woods on park trails. Regarding litter such as beer cans and pop bottles, pick up what you can.

Finally, hunting is prohibited in the areas discussed in this book, but fishing is allowed. Camping and swimming are sometimes permitted as noted at the outset of each chapter. Most of the parks and watershed lands are open from dawn until dusk, but some sections of the state parks (Orange Grove, McKeldin, and Bunker Hill in Hereford), as well as the county parks (Oregon Ridge and Fort Howard), open at 10:00 A.M.

1

PATAPSCO VALLEY STATE PARK
Orange Grove and Avalon

Walking and ski touring — 5 miles (8 kilometers). From the overlook and steep bluff at Orange Grove to the bridge at Avalon on a wide riverside path. Return by River Road or on a footpath that winds in and out of the ravines along the side of the valley. Cross back over the river on the swinging bridge at Orange Grove. Picnicking and camping facilities are available near the Hilton Avenue entrance of the park; other picnic facilities are at Avalon. During winter telephone beforehand in order to check whether the Hilton entrance is open on weekdays. Managed by the Maryland Park Service (747-6602).

BETWEEN WOODSTOCK (west of Baltimore) and tidewater at Elkridge, the Patapsco River falls more than two hundred feet in a distance of seventeen miles, much of it through a steep-sided valley. The potential of this stretch of river for water power was not lost on the ironmongers, millers, textile manufacturers, and other early industrialists of the 18th and 19th centuries, and during that period many dams and factories were built in the narrow valley, notably at Elysville (now Daniels), Ellicotts Upper and Lower Mills, Oella, Ilchester, Orange Grove, and Avalon. This and the following three walks pass these sites. A few are still active mills. Others are just ruins or

stretches of wooded valley where whole factory villages have been obliterated by fire and flood and whose names survive only as designations for different sections of the Patapsco Valley State Park.

Avalon is one of these lost towns. It got its start in the 1760's when Caleb Dorsey, ironmaster and owner of Elkridge Furnace, built a forge upstream from his furnace for fashioning implements from the pig iron that he produced. According to the 19th-century memoirs of Martha Ellicott Tyson (a descendant of the Ellicotts of Ellicott City), the only iron tools made in Baltimore County prior to the American Revolution were crowbars produced at Dorsey's Forge, called Avalon. All other tools were imported, as was intended under the British Mercantile System by which the colonies were to provide raw materials to England and to purchase finished goods in return.

During the Revolution a mill to produce rolled, slit, and sheet iron was established at Avalon by William Whetcroft of Annapolis, who had received a government loan voted by the Convention, Maryland's revolutionary legislature. Whetcroft also had a contract to manufacture muskets. His lease with Dorsey's son Edward (known as Iron Head Ned) stipulated that Dorsey would raise the dam at Avalon an additional foot and dig a race to Whetcroft's mill for water power to run the bellows and other machinery; in exchange Whetcroft not only would pay rent for use of the site but would also buy all of his raw iron from Edward Dorsey, who later purchased the Whetcroft mill for himself.

After Edward Dorsey's death in 1815, the Avalon property was purchased at auction by two members of the enterprising Ellicott family, who then conveyed the mill to the newly-chartered Avalon Company owned by seven Ellicott partners. By 1820 the Ellicott iron works — one at Avalon and another a few miles upstream at Ellicott City — were listed together in the census as having between them 4 rolling mills, 6 pair of rollers with the necessary furnaces, and 24 nail machines. They employed more than sixty hands to produce bar iron, sheet iron, boiler plate, nails, and brads. Later the works were expanded to

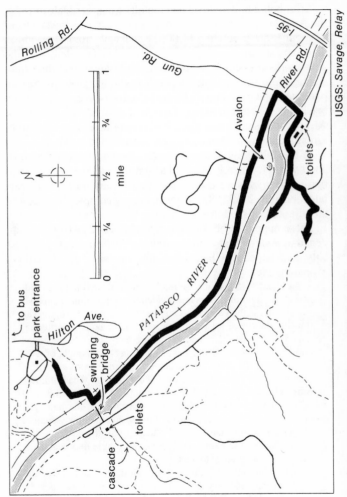

USGS: Savage, Relay

make barrel hoops and to roll rails for the Baltimore & Ohio Railroad.

After being pulled down and rebuilt on a larger scale in 1854, the Avalon nail factory reached its peak under new management in about 1856, producing 44,000 kegs of nails from 44 machines driven by steam. In a panoramic print of Avalon dated 1855, the iron works are shown as two long buildings resembling train sheds side by side, standing parallel with the river on the east bank near the present park bridge. The roofs were supported on brick piers. Four tall smokestacks rose between the mill sheds. Around the factory was a small village of at least twenty structures, including a church, a school, stores, and mill houses.

In the following years, however, the nail factory declined, and by 1864, when it was sold again, the advertisements stated that the works were used solely as a rolling mill. Four years later, on July 24, 1868, the entire factory complex and most of the village vanished in a few hours.

There appear to be no contemporary accounts of what happened at Avalon that morning, but the events at nearby Ellicott City, as recalled by Charles F. Kreh, who was there at the time, give some idea:

At about 9:15 o'clock the mail train from Baltimore arrived, and at that hour there was little evidence or intimation of impending disaster in the Patapsco. Only a lowering of the clouds and an unusual darkness, together with some fierce bolts of lightning, appeared to cast their shadows before them and to indicate the coming of a storm. But, as yet, few if any had thought of what was in store for them. Soon, however, came reports of terrible cloudbursts in various places west of the Ellicotts. The Baltimore train left the station and had only reached Union Mills about a mile distant, when it was met by an avalanche of water. The bounds of the river were already broken and only the weight of the train held it to the tracks. Fortunately for the passengers, it stood close by the mountain side, and they were thus enabled to clamber up and return to the city.

Hardly had a few minutes elapsed before the mad waters (in all their intensity and fury and without any warning) burst upon the good people of Ellicotts living along the river course on the Baltimore County side, and almost in a twinkling their homes were surrounded and all avenues of escape cut off. Then began scenes that almost beggar description, many of them pitiful and heartrending. The waters, filled with logs and trees and debris of all kinds, arose as if by magic and seemed to gloat in their power of fierce destruction. Opposite the railroad station across the Patapsco stood a row of houses, some brick, some frame and others stone, extending over a space of about 1,000 feet from the bridge to the mill structure . . . and in a remarkably short time these were seen to begin to crumble from the beating of the waves against them. Now could be seen the dwellers breaking through the roofs from house to house and barely escaping the collapse of their homes. The last house in the row was a brick building owned by William Partridge and in this 30-odd persons sought refuge. Many were the prayers that went up to the Most High from those looking on from the opposite shore that this house might be spared, but it was not to be, and soon all were engulfed and swallowed up in the angry waters. School children, who had come across the river in the early morning, stood on the banks and saw their parents go to their watery graves.

The flood crest reached forty feet above normal. Workers fled the factories as the riverside buildings were inundated. The massive Granite Cotton Mill in Ellicott City collapsed into the torrent, taking with it one man who had been too slow to leave. Bodies from Ellicott City were recovered near Baltimore, twelve miles downstream. Those of one man and his wife and child were found caught in the top of a tree. In all about fifty people drowned that morning in the Patapsco Valley.

At Avalon no lives were lost but the factory slumped into the river. Only a few houses survived; one stone dwelling still stands on high ground near the railroad crossing above the park bridge. The old factory-like brick building nearby is not a remnant of the Avalon mill but a former pumping station built about 1910 for the Baltimore County Water and Electric Company, which for a period maintained a dam and reservoir at Avalon.

Since 1868 the Patapsco Valley has experienced lesser floods (as it always had) on a more or less regular basis. Tropical storm Agnes in 1972, however, was of a different order of magnitude:

it was comparable to the flood a century earlier. Beginning June 21, the storm lumbered across Maryland in three days of almost constant rain. At Ellicott City one of the early Ellicott houses that had survived the prior flood was toppled. Over $1,800,000 in damage occurred in the Patapsco Valley State Park alone. At Avalon the high water washed out the east end of the dam over which the river used to flow. The park bridge was destroyed, as were most other small bridges. Shelters were swept away and the swinging footbridge at Orange Grove was pulled down. The former Avalon pumping station, at that time used as a park maintenance building, was flooded to the top of its twelve-foot doors and later 1½ feet of mud were shoveled out. Between Ilchester and Avalon the current ate away long stretches of River Road and the B&O railbed, and the large sanitary sewer that runs down the valley was ruptured in four places. The thickets of young trees and brush that now stand along the same stretch of river indicate that much of the former vegetation was stripped away. One resident said that the full-sized trees below his house resembled shrubbery barely protruding above the water. Among the victims drowned in the flood was a man whose canoe (he was out for fun) snagged in the top of a utility pole.

Since 1972 much of the damage has been repaired. The swinging bridge has been replaced and new shelters have been built. River Road has also been reconstructed between Avalon and Orange Grove. In the meantime, however, park visitors have become accustomed to the pleasant circuit walk free of automobile traffic up and down both banks of the river, so that the park staff now intends to experiment with barring motor vehicles from the road above Avalon. If, after walking through this area, you favor closing the road to motor vehicles on weekends or at other times (as is currently done with parts of Loch Raven Road), call the park superintendent's office at 747-6602 or write to : Patapsco Valley State Park, 1100 Hilton Avenue, Baltimore, Md. 21228.

BUS: From downtown take the MTA Catonsville bus (#8) via Fayette Street and Frederick Road west through

ORANGE GROVE/AVALON

Catonsville. Get off where Rolling Road intersects Frederick Road from the south opposite Hillcrest Elementary School. You will know that your stop is coming after passing over the Beltway and through the Catonsville business district.

From the bus stop walk south on Rolling Road about 200 yards and then continue straight on Hilton Avenue where Rolling Road veers left. Follow Hilton Avenue 1.5 miles to the Patapsco Valley State Park entrance on the right 100 yards past the park maintenance center.

AUTOMOBILE: From Exit 13 off the Beltway (I-695) take Frederick Road (Route 144) west 1.2 miles through Catonsville. Turn left where Rolling Road intersects Frederick Road from the south opposite Hillcrest Elementary School. Follow Rolling Road south 0.1 mile and then continue straight on Hilton Avenue 1.5 miles to the Patapsco Valley State Park entrance on the right, 100 yards past the park maintenance center. On weekends and holidays during April through September, there is an entrance fee of $3 per car (as of 1981).

The park can also be reached from Washington Boulevard (Route 1). Turn onto South Street a few hundred yards east of the river and follow the park road under the Thomas Viaduct and high I-95 bridge. At a "T" intersection turn either way to reach large parking areas. Pick up the circuit walk where the route passes through the Avalon area and across the Avalon bridge. This approach avoids the steep bluff that is encountered by hikers starting from and returning to the park entrance off Hilton Avenue. For ski touring, start at Avalon.

THE WALK: With your back to the ranger station at the park entrance off Hilton Avenue, follow the circle road left or clockwise one-quarter of the way around the loop to an intersection with a road leading to a parking lot. This intersection marks the point where a wide dirt path leaves

11

the outer edge of the loop. Follow the path downhill for several hundred yards past picnic sites and through the woods to an overlook above the river and railroad tracks. The narrow valley bottom along this section of the river used to be occupied by the dam, flour mill, and village of Orange Grove, discussed in the next chapter.

Descend very steeply to the left. After checking for oncoming trains, cross the tracks and descend to the riverside path and footbridge. If a train on the siding blocks the way, detour to the right two hundred yards around the end of the siding. Allow ample leeway in case the train starts to move.

With the river on your right follow the path downstream away from the footbridge, which you will cross on your return. At one point you will pass on the right the crumpled and punctured hulk of a steel tank truck that was tumbled down the river from somewhere upstream during tropical storm Agnes in the summer of 1972.

Continue downstream through a parking area. Pass a pond on the right and a small underpass on the left. Follow the asphalt drive to the park entrance.

At a four-way intersection note one of the few surviving Avalon houses uphill to the left and the old brick pumping station straight ahead. Turn right across the old millrace and then across the river. Immediately beyond the bridge, turn right off the road and follow the edge of the field past the former bridge abutment and along the river bank upstream. Eventually, curve left to the road and follow it upstream, with the river on the right. Walk in the pedestrian lane on the side of the road nearest the river.

For an easy walk upstream along the river bank to the pedestrian bridge, follow the road. However, if the traffic is disagreeable, a pleasant but somewhat strenuous footpath follows the rim of the valley, with excellent views during the leafless seasons. To join this footpath, follow the riverside road upstream to the remains of the old Avalon dam, with the pond on the opposite shore. One

Swinging bridge, Orange Grove

hundred yards upstream from the dam abutment, fork left onto a gravel road. Follow the ravine uphill 160 yards, then fork right onto a less worn path. Continue up the ravine. As you approach the crest of the hill where the path begins to level, turn very sharply on a footpath intersecting from the right. Follow this footpath up, down, and around the heads of several ravines. At a particularly large ravine, descend steeply as the path winds down and around to the left, then ascend straight up the other side. Turn right at a "T" intersection. Descend into the next ravine and go up the other side, passing above a stone and concrete shelter. Descend into another ravine to the remains of an asphalt road. Fork left and follow the footpath across a stream, past a small pavilion, and along the side of the valley. Climb to join a wider path and follow it downhill to the riverside road.

Continue upstream to the swinging footbridge. A few yards upstream from the end of the bridge, a path marked by a flight of stone steps leads 300 yards to an attractive cascade and wading pool.

Cross the swinging bridge and climb back to your starting point at the top of the valley.

2

PATAPSCO VALLEY STATE PARK
Orange Grove and Ilchester

Walking — 4 miles (6.4 kilometers). From the Hilton entrance to the old but still active mill at Ilchester on well-worn footpaths and little-used roads. The route threads through ravines and along a steep ridge above the Patapsco Valley. Return on a riverside path past the Bloede Dam to the cascade, swinging bridge, and ruins at Orange Grove. During winter telephone beforehand in order to check whether the Hilton entrance is open on weekdays. Managed by the Maryland Park Service (747-6602).

THE MASSIVE STONE WALL shown on page 17 is situated on the bank of the Patapsco River at Orange Grove. It was once part of the Patapsco Flour Mill "C", which in 1900 was called the largest flour mill east of Minneapolis.

The dam, mill, and village at Orange Grove were located in the narrow valley bottom below the present-day entrance to the state park off Hilton Avenue. According to the memoirs of a former Orange Grove resident — Thomas LeRoy Phillips, whose father was superintendent of the mill from 1891 to 1904 — "the subdued rumble of the mill was heard from early Monday morning to late Saturday evening; the muffled roar of water pouring over the high wooden dam was unbroken; and long freight trains rolled by day and night.'' Powered by three horizontal water wheels and a Corliss steam engine (of which the day engineer was so fond that he called his son Corliss), the mill produced twelve to fifteen thousand barrels of flour a day. Two of its better known brands were Orange Grove and Patapsco Superlative Patent; the latter was the highest grade, made from the whitest part of the kernel.

A flour mill was first constructed at Orange Grove in 1856, when George Worthington and George Baily bought land there on both sides of the river. According to the deed, the property included parts of tracts known as ''Talbot's Last Shift,'' ''Small Bit,'' ''Joseph and Jacob's Invention,'' and all of ''Vortex.'' It is thought that the new mill and small mill village became known as Orange Grove due to the Osage orange trees that were common in the area. In 1860 Worthington and Baily sold the entire property to the C. A. Gambrill Manufacturing Company, which had also taken over the Ellicott family's mill farther upstream. The Gambrill mill at Ellicott City was termed ''Mill A.'' ''Mill B'' was in Baltimore City, and ''Mill C'' was at Orange Grove.

In 1873 Gambrill added the Corliss steam engine and boilers to supplement water power at Orange Grove. Ten years later the mill's stone grist wheels were replaced by modern steel rollers. The mill building measured 150 by 175 feet. By 1900 it had six stories, four of brick topped by two more of frame and metal siding. A massive rectangular grain elevator eight stories high flanked the mill on its upstream side, and on the downstream side there was a tall, tapering, square smokestack and a three-story structure housing the Corliss engine, coal bins, and a dynamo that generated electricity to light the mill and the nearby superintendent's house.

The entire mill complex was crowded onto a shelf of land between the railroad and a high retaining wall along the river. There was so little room to spare that the former Gun Road (now the riverside path) used to pass through the building in an arched

passageway. Trains unloaded grain and coal and picked up flour at the third floor level, since the mill and elevator were set into the hillside. A wooden dam about ten feet high and slightly curved against the current created a millpond stretching upstream as far as Ilchester.

On the opposite bank from the mill a small company-owned village of at least seven houses and a one-room school and church was strung out along the river where a parking lot and restrooms are now located. Then as now the river was spanned by a swinging bridge, which was snagged and pulled down by an ice jam in January, 1904, and again washed out by tropical storm Agnes in 1972. A community hand pump provided water. Horse-drawn grocery and butcher carts supplied some food; other shopping entailed a short train ride to Ellicott City or Baltimore on one of the twelve passenger trains that stopped daily at Orange Grove. And, on every third Sunday church services were conducted by a traveling reverend who also preached at Elkridge and at Locust Chapel near Ilchester.

The mill at Orange Grove operated until May 1, 1905, when it was gutted by fire. The remains of the brick walls were torn down, but the dam abutment and large sections of the stone foundations still remain and are passed by the route described below.

BUS: From downtown take the MTA Catonsville bus (#8) via Fayette Street and Frederick Road west through Catonsville. Get off where Rolling Road intersects Frederick Road from the south opposite Hillcrest Elementary School. You will know that your stop is coming after passing over the Beltway and through the Catonsville business district.

From the bus stop walk south on Rolling Road about 200 yards and then continue straight on Hilton Avenue where Rolling Road veers left. Follow Hilton Avenue 1.5 miles to the Patapsco Valley State Park entrance on the right, 100 yards past the park maintenance center.

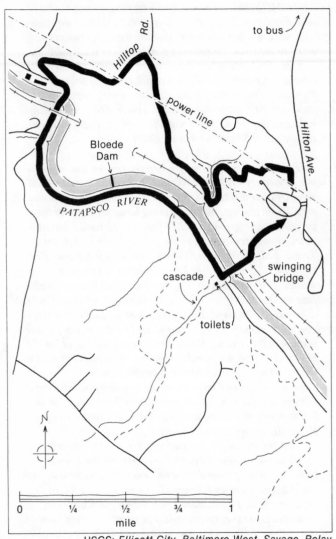

USGS: *Ellicott City, Baltimore West, Savage, Relay*

*AUTOMOBILE: From Exit 13 off the Beltway (I-695)
take Frederick Road (Route 144) west 1.2 miles through
Catonsville. Turn left where Rolling Road intersects Frederick Road from the south opposite Hillcrest Elementary
School. Follow Rolling Road south 0.1 mile and then
continue straight on Hilton Avenue 1.5 miles to the
Patapsco Valley State Park entrance on the right, 100
yards after the park maintenance center. On weekends and
holidays during April through September, there is an entrance fee of $3 per car (as of 1981).*

*THE WALK: With your back to the ranger station at the
park entrance off Hilton Avenue, follow the looping road
right or counterclockwise. Turn right at the first opportunity. From the left end of a parking lot under a power line,
follow a white gravel road 75 yards to a broad footpath
marked with red blazes on the left (the Saw Mill Branch
Trail). Follow the path downhill and across a power line
right-of-way. Fork right 25 yards after re-entering the
woods. Follow the path straight as it slopes down along the
side of the hill. At a "T" intersection turn left uphill, then
downhill to the right. Fifty yards past the foot of the slope,
veer right downhill on the red-blazed trail. Continue to the
bottom of the ravine. With a stream on the right, follow the
ravine downhill half a mile. Eventually the path appears to
vanish at a gravel bar above a jumble of trees in the
streambed. Detour left around the log jam and follow the
stream to a large stone arch culvert. Climb steeply to the
left to reach the railroad tracks overlooking the Patapsco
River. Be on the lookout for trains.*

*With the Patapsco on your left, follow the tracks 60
yards to where several paths emerge from the woods.
Climb very steeply up the narrow ridge path to the left, with
the Patapsco Valley falling off on your left and the ravine
on your right. Two hundred yards after the path levels,
some rocks on the left provide a particularly good view of
the valley, the Bloede Dam, and the road on the opposite
bank by which you will return.*

Continue on the path away from the valley, under a power line, and through the woods to Hilltop Road. Follow Hilltop Road left back to the power line, past some houses, then steeply downhill. Turn sharply left downhill past stone houses overlooking Simkins Industries, Inc.

This is Ilchester: a dam and paper mill, a bridge, and a few stone mill houses up the hill. In 1837 George and William Morris, two Scottish brothers, established their Thistle Mills here for making cotton print. Thistle Road still links Frederick Road with the river just beyond the upstream end of the mill complex. By 1900 the mill had been converted to spinning silk before being reconverted for the manufacture of cotton duck and tire fabric. Then in 1922 the Bartgis brothers of Baltimore moved their paper carton business into the old Thistle plant, which has since passed through several more hands. The factory now recycles wastepaper to produce paper board, the kind of cardboard used in cereal boxes and cigarette cartons.

Turn left on River Road and follow it across the river and under the railroad. Turn left onto an abandoned and barricaded asphalt road just beyond the intersection with Bonnie Branch Road.

This section of River Road was washed away by the flood during tropical storm Agnes in 1972. The stone arch and abutment at the river's edge are the remains of the B&O Patterson Viaduct, destroyed by the flood of 1868.

With the river on your left, head downsteam on the remains of the road. When it disappears, follow the rough footpath along the river. Pick up the road again by the Bloede Dam, built in 1907. Generators formerly were housed in rooms within the dam, which was abandoned in 1927.

With the river on your left, follow the remains of River Road downstream to the swinging bridge, where the vil-

lage of Orange Grove was located. A few yards upstream from the end of the bridge, a path marked by a flight of stone steps leads 300 yards to an attractive cascade and wading pool.

From the middle of the swinging bridge, the stone abutment of the old wooden Orange Grove dam is visible about a hundred yards upsteam on the west bank of the river. On the east bank the stone foundations of the former mill and grain elevator stretch upstream seventy-five yards along the railroad embankment. The walls are obscured by trees and are best examined close up. The small "doorway" in the stonework immediately above the end of the footbridge may have been the opening to the chute through which coal was dumped from the railroad siding.

After crossing the footbridge, climb straight up the embankment to the railroad tracks. After checking for oncoming trains, cross the tracks to the foot of the bluff. If the way is blocked by a train on the siding, detour 200 yards upstream around the end of the siding and back along the foot of the bluff. Allow ample leeway in case the train starts to move. Climb half-left up the steep path to the rim of the valley. Follow the wide path uphill to the looping road and parking area where you started.

3

ELLICOTT CITY AND OELLA

Walking — 1.5 to 4 miles (2.4 to 6.4 kilometers), depending on whether you continue by foot to Oella. The narrow streets, stone store fronts, specialty shops, and railroad station museum of Maryland's leading 19th-century mill town. Nearby is Oella, a self-contained mill community.

As A NAME AND ANACHRONISM, Ellicott "City" is perhaps on a par with Baltimore "Towne." The Ellicott City charter was revoked, in fact, by the General Assembly in 1935, after a half-century of economic decline in the Patapsco Valley following the great flood of 1868. Today, despite a glossy new varnish of antique chic, the "city" retains much of the flavor of the mill town, quarries, and early railroad terminus of its origin. Its stone and frame buildings are jammed along a narrow valley where Frederick Road crosses the river. A mile upstream on the opposite bank is the industrial village of Oella, a remarkable concentration of 19th-century mill housing.

In 1772 Joseph, Andrew, and John Ellicott, Quaker brothers from Bucks County, Pennsylvania, bought land on both sides of the Patapsco River for two miles above and below the present

site of Ellicott City. Their newly-acquired stretch of valley was uninhabited, uncultivated, and inaccessible except by footpath. The attraction lay in the steep gradient of the river, for the Ellicotts' purchase included the right to impound water for power. In 1774 the brothers also purchased an existing dam and mill for grinding corn four miles upstream, where the river was crossed by the then Frederick Road (now *Old* Frederick Road), at that time a horsepath for pack animals.

Prior to their purchases in the Patapsco Valley, Andrew and John Ellicott had traveled on horseback over the middle counties of Maryland between the Patapsco and the Blue Ridge. They had concluded from their tour of inspection that the region was suited for growing wheat and had ample water power for grinding grain. Tobacco was then the exclusive cash crop near Baltimore, but the European demand for American tobacco had slumped, payment from European dealers was slow, and yields were declining as the soil became depleted. Also, as a matter of agricultural heritage, the new German settlers in central Maryland (where Frederick had been named for the kings of Prussia) preferred to grow wheat. In consequence, the Ellicotts perceived that a regional grain market was in the making. Between 1749 and 1774 the export of wheat and flour from Annapolis had already increased by nearly 600 percent, and the growth of wheat exporting at Baltimore had been even more dramatic.

From the outset Joseph Ellicott concentrated his attention on the improvement of the upstream site on Frederick Road, which became known as the Upper Mills. John, Andrew, and Andrew's sons undertook development of the lower stretch of river. Their household goods, tools, and farm implements were brought by boat from Philadelphia to Elkridge Landing, which at that time was the head of navigation on the Patapsco River and, in comparison with other towns on the Chesapeake's western shore, a major tobacco port from which ships sailed directly to England. From Elkridge the Ellicotts' possessions were carried by wagon and then by wheelbarrow on a footpath along the river to the new settlement. Even the wagons themselves had to be disassembled and carried in.

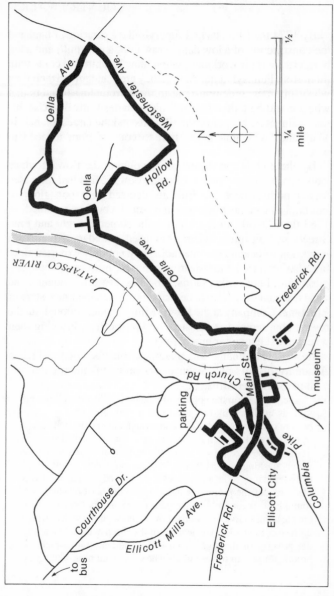

USGS: Ellicott City

By 1774 the Ellicotts had supervised the clearing of land and the construction of a low dam, a saw mill, a grist mill, and a log barracks for their workmen, whom they had hired to come with them from Pennsylvania. At first they grew and milled their own wheat in order to demonstrate to the surrounding planters that wheat could be cultivated and sold. Charles Carroll of Carrollton, a financial backer of the Ellicotts and the largest planter in Maryland, was among the first to convert from tobacco to wheat.

By the end of the American Revolution the flow of wheat from nearby plantations to Ellicotts Lower Mills had increased to the point where the Ellicotts decided to export flour to England as soon as trade with the British could be resumed. In 1783 the Ellicotts built a wharf at the corner of Light and Pratt Streets in Baltimore, where they used a dredge of their own invention to deepen the channel. They not only exported flour but also imported English ironware, tea, mirrors, dinner sets, glassware, linen, silks, satins, brocades, groceries, liquors, and wines, which they sold to the planters through their new store of Ellicott & Company at the Lower Mills. Planters throughout the region congregated at the store and post office, bringing their wheat in exchange for purchases.

In 1791 Ferdinand M. Bayard, a member of the French Academy of Arts and Sciences, recorded his impression of a visit to the Lower Mills:

> The river, upon the borders of which Mr. Ellicott has built his mill, is enclosed by two chains of uncultivated hills . . . . The bottom of the river, whose channel can hardly be decried, is full of broken rocks which the waters have not yet worked smooth. Some masses are raised above the surface of the river, whose water, dashing against them, keep up continually a dull noise, truly sepulchral. The advantages to be derived from a mill in this place render the proprietor insensible to the horrors which surround him. It can only be a regard for pecuniary interest which enables him to live undisturbed by the noise of the waters which dash over the rocks. The leaness of the sheep and cattle attest to the poverty of the soil. A miserable garden, from which the productions seem forced; fields where the scantiness of the grain

leaves the soil exposed; plains incapable of producing a middling sized oak; such is the melancholy aspect presented by the country from Baltimore to Ellicott's Mills.

In time the Ellicotts erected iron-smelting furnaces, forges, rolling mills, and nail factories in their stretch of the Patapsco Valley. Other mills were added later for the production of copper sheathing. A Quaker meeting house and school were built. After reading an article in a horticultural journal and conducting their own experiments with plaster, the Ellicotts instructed the surrounding planters in the use of lime as a fertilizer to restore the exhausted soil. They imported blocks of gypsum from Nova Scotia and ground it for fertilizer. At their own expense they constructed bridges and a road east to Baltimore and, with the assistance of Charles Carroll, west to Carroll's vast Doughoregan Manor. Other planters helped to extend the road to Frederick, opening the new wheat country of the interior to Ellicotts Lower Mills. In 1804 the Frederick Turnpike between Baltimore and the middle of the state was established through the Lower Mills, supplanting the old Frederick Road through the Upper Mills. The turnpike soon was linked with the Ohio Valley by the National Road through Cumberland and Wheeling, so that by 1818, when the settlement numbered about three thousand people, the country's most important land thoroughfare passed through Ellicotts Lower Mills.

During the same period granite quarrying became a significant industry. Between 1806 and 1821 granite for Baltimore Cathedral — at the time one of the nation's most significant structures because of its large size and distinguished neoclassic design — was hauled from Ellicotts Lower Mills along the Frederick Turnpike in huge wagons drawn by nine yoke of oxen.

Ellicotts Lower Mills received another boost in 1827, when the Baltimore & Ohio Railroad was incorporated by several leading Baltimore merchants and bankers. They feared that the Erie Canal, completed in 1825, and the newly planned Chesapeake & Ohio Canal, with its terminus in Georgetown, would each divert commerce with the Great Lakes region and the Ohio Valley away from Baltimore. The first leg of the experimental railroad was laid up the Patapsco Valley, and Ellicotts Lower Mills was selected as its inland terminus until the line was extended farther westward.

During the next forty years Ellicotts Lower Mills continued to grow and prosper, although in the aftermath of the financial panic of 1837, one branch of the Ellicott family, "trading under the name of Jonathan Ellicott & Sons, being embarrassed in their circumstances and largely indebted to many individuals" (as recited in the deed of trust), was forced to convey the flour mill to trustees for the benefit of their creditors. Colonel Charles Carroll III acquired the mill in partnership with Charles A. Gambrill, who gradually became the firm's principal. The mill continued to be owned by the C. A. Gambrill Manufacturing Company until 1923, and during that period it was rebuilt at least twice after being destroyed by flood or damaged by fire. Most of the currently existing mill structure, still in use today, dates from 1917.

In 1840 Ellicotts Lower Mills was selected as the site for the courthouse for the new Howard District of what was then Anne Arundel County, and in 1851 it was made the county seat when Howard County was organized. The Lower Mills became Ellicott City with the granting of a municipal charter in 1867. The next year, however, much of the city's industry was destroyed in a devastating flash flood, as described in Chapter 1. Although some of the mills were rebuilt, many were not, and the community never fully recovered economically.

BUS: From the Trailways Bus Terminal at 210 West Fayette Street, take the Columbia bus west on Route 40. Buy a ticket to the Golden Triangle but tell the driver that you want to get off at Rogers Avenue (Route 99), and that you will be returning from the same intersection later in the day. You will know that your stop is coming as the bus descends the second hill after crossing the Patapsco River. For the return trip, be sure that you know the time of

*arrival for the bus that you plan to take and that you flag
the bus as it approaches. For detailed schedule information, call 442-1330 or 752-2115.*

*From Route 40 follow Rogers Avenue south toward
Ellicott City. Continue straight on Courthouse Drive to the
large parking lot in back of the Howard County Courthouse. The total distance is one mile.*

*AUTOMOBILE: From Route 40 the Howard County
Courthouse (where the walk begins) is one mile south from
the intersection with Rogers Avenue (Route 99). Follow
Rogers Avenue and continue straight on Courthouse Drive
to the large parking area in back of the courthouse.*

*THE WALK: From the courthouse parking lot head to-
ward the golden dome of the courthouse complex. Pass to
the left of the buildings, and then turn right in front of the
courthouse.*

The Howard County Courthouse was built in 1840-43 on the
hill overlooking the main valley of Ellicotts Lower Mills, supposedly in order to put the court at a distance from the unseemly
sounds and odors of the livestock that regularly were driven in
herds along the Frederick Turnpike to Baltimore. To visit the
handsome principal courtroom, you should take the stairs just
inside the front entrance and then (quietly) enter through the
double doors at the top landing. The courthouse is open 8:30 to
4:30 on weekdays.

*From the front steps of the courthouse, continue down-
hill into the valley on Courthouse Road. Turn left on Main
Street and follow it down past the intersection with Old
Columbia Pike. Continue to the depot square at the foot of
Main Street.*

The large building with the ironwork porch at 8202 Main
Street is the Howard House, built as a hotel about 1850. Because

it was carved into the hillside with its back door at ground level on the third floor, the hotel's central stairs became a thoroughfare between Main Street and Church Road on the way to and from the courthouse. The first floor, as later expanded, had a bar, a lunchroom, and an ice cream parlor. The second floor included a dining room for hotel guests and a separate banqueting hall. Following the construction of the railroad, tourists flocked to the town in order to combine the novelty of a train ride with a country excursion. Also, the granting of a municipal charter gave Ellicott City the right to license the sale of liquor. The city became the only "wet spot" in Howard County and the site of lavish parties.

Four doors down from the Howard House is the Walker-Chandler house, built about 1790. It has served successively as a private residence, a boot-maker's shop, offices, funeral home, tavern and dive, then offices again, before becoming Ellicott's Country Store.

At 8046 Main Street is the former Colonial Inn and Opera House, purportedly where John Wilkes Booth made his debut. Another prominent inn was the Patapsco Hotel at 8004-8026 Main Street, immediately adjacent to the railroad tracks. Rather than depositing the hotel's guests at the depot across the street, the train made another stop at a platform along the side of the hotel's second floor, so that guests could enter the hotel directly from the railroad carriages.

From the depot square continue east on Main Street under the railroad to the bridge over the Patapsco River.

The site of the original Ellicotts Lower Mills is now occupied by the Wilkins-Rogers flour mill and silos at the bend in the river downstream from the Fredrick Road bridge. Most of the early settlement was on the east bank of the river but was destroyed by the flood of 1868. The row of houses where thirty-six people died (as discussed in Chapter 1) stood between the mill and higher ground. Opposite the mill near the Frederick Road are the remains of the stone house of George Ellicott, a son of Andrew Ellicott.

33

Back on the west bank of the Patapsco, between the river and the railroad, is another old stone structure, believed to have been built originally as a house for mill hands. For a period during the 19th century it served as Radcliffe's Emporium, a general store. Neighboring houses upstream were swept away by the flood of 1868. The bridge abutments above the Frederick Road bridge mark where the Ellicott City trolley line used to cross the river.

The mill village of Oella, mentioned at the outset of this chapter, is located on Oella Avenue about three-quarters of a mile upstream from the eastern end of the Frederick Road bridge. If you want to visit Oella, you can walk from the bridge and then return or (if you have a car) wait until the end of your Ellicott City tour and then drive to Oella. In either case, information concerning Oella is at the end of the chapter.

Return to the depot square and railroad station in Ellicott City.

The B&O station dates from 1831, when the railroad first reached Ellicotts Lower Mills. Because the station was the end of the line, a turntable was built to rotate the engine for the trip back to Baltimore. The building has been restored to its early 19th-century appearance and now houses the B&O Railroad Station Museum. Call 461-1944 for information regarding the museum's hours and admission fees.

From the curved wall in front of the Railroad Museum, cross the street and enter the alley opposite. Turn right over Tiber Run and then left on Main Street. Turn left up Old Columbia Pike and continue to Tongue Row, a group of four stone houses (now shops) built by a Mr. Tongue for mill hands in the early 1800's.

From Tongue Row descend on the narrow stairs between the buildings to a parking lot. Turn right. Cross Main Street and climb Church Street past the former firehouse, where leather buckets and other hand equipment

*were once kept. Turn left opposite the Emory United
Methodist Church. Turn left again to climb past the small
offices of Lawyers Row and the former First Presbyterian
Church, now headquarters of the Howard County Historical Society. Turn right past the courthouse and return to
the parking lot.*

As noted earlier, the village of Oella, which in physical terms
remains an enclave of unmodernized mill housing surrounding
the former textile plant, is located on the east bank of the
Patapsco River about three-quarters of a mile upstream from
Frederick Road. Oella got its start in 1808 when the Ellicotts
sold two miles of land along the river to the Union Manufacturing Company of Maryland, the first corporation to be chartered
by the state legislature. The Union dam (now breached at its
western end) is located about 1.5 miles upstream from the
village and just below the Route 40 bridge. From the dam a
millrace, constructed with slave labor and said to be one of the
longest races in the country feeding a single mill, runs along the
eastern bank of the river to Oella, creating a vertical drop at the
mill of nearly fifty feet. The mill generated its own power until
the construction of Liberty Dam in 1954-55 diminished the flow
of water.

For a period the Union mill at Oella was among the nation's
largest makers of cotton goods, but in 1889 financial difficulties
forced its sale to William J. Dickey of the Dickeyville mills,
who converted the plant to making woolen fabric and renamed
the community Oella, supposedly an Indian name for the area.
The original mill burned down in 1918 but was replaced with a
new one. The plant reached its peak in the 1950's, when it
employed five hundred workers producing fancy woolen fabrics
for men's sport coats and suits. In the 1960's, however, the
upsurge in imported textiles and synthetics engulfed domestic
woolen manufacturers. The decline at Oella became even more
precipitous with the advent of double-knit fabrics that could not
be produced on the machinery used there. In 1972 the plant was
closed and sold. Parts of it are now leased as a warehouse and
furniture outlet.

35

The future of Oella even as a residential community has been problematic for years because there is no public water or sewer system. Raw sewage from the former mill housing is pumped into leaky cesspools and septic tanks. Many residents still get their drinking water from a community pump, and some private wells have been closed because of contamination.

Baltimore County now plans to install water and sewer lines through the rocky terrain at a cost of more than $6 million. To justify the expense some plans call for the construction of additional housing and the conversion of the mill to offices, light industry, and conceivably apartments, restaurants, and specialty shops, like those across the river in Ellicott City. There is little likelihood, however, that tenants living in the old mill housing, some of whom are descendants of three or four generations of mill employees, will be able to survive the rise in rent resulting from the increase in local real estate values, taxes, and hook-up fees that water and sewer lines will entail. Planners anticipate that many of these families will be displaced, if not by higher rents then by the sale of the old houses to individual owners after water and sewer lines are installed.

To reach Oella from Ellicott City, cross the Patapsco River on Frederick Road (i.e., Main Street). Turn left immediately on Oella Avenue and follow it past the low shelf of land that at the beginning of the 19th century was the site of the Ellicott Iron Works and later the Granite Cotton Mill, destroyed in the flood of 1868. Follow Oella Avenue along the side of the valley above the river and past mill housing on the right built between 1830 and 1840. Turn right at the large mill and then sharp left at an intersection by the former Methodist Church so as to continue around the back of the factory. Follow the road past more mill housing. Curve right and continue past intersections with Pleasant Hill Road and Race Road. Turn right at Westchester Avenue. Eventually turn right downhill on Hollow Road. Fork left past the mill to return to Frederick Road by the way you came.

4

PATAPSCO VALLEY STATE PARK
Ellicotts Upper Mills and Daniels

*Walking and ski touring — 4 to 8 miles (6.4 to 12.9 kilometers)
depending on how far you continue past Daniels. From the Old
Frederick Road bridge (site of now-vanished Ellicotts Upper
Mills) westward along the winding Patapsco Valley to the dam
and ruined mill complex at Daniels. Although the mill buildings
at Daniels are privately owned and are closed to the public, they
are easily viewed from the park path. A spur trail leads a short
distance to the stone remains of St. Stanislaus Kostka Church.
From Daniels, the broad trail continues upstream and eventually turns into a narrow footpath through a particularly isolated
section of the valley. Managed by the Maryland Park Service
(747-6602).*

FIVE HUNDRED FIFTY ACRES fronting on the Patapsco
River. A factory complex consisting of a three-story stone mill,
48 by 230 feet, and various larger but lower brick and cement-
block structures for the manufacture of heavy canvas, denim,
industrial belting, and hose. A concrete dam furnishing 400
horsepower and generating surplus electricity that was sold to
the Baltimore Gas and Electric Company. A post office, a
community hall, and a general store. And 118 single-family,
two-family, and rowhouse dwellings, most of them brick, averaging five rooms each, many without interior plumbing. This

in 1940 was Alberton, before that Elysville and since renamed Daniels, for three generations the company town of James S. Gary & Sons. On November 23, 1940, the entire town was sold — houses, factory, and machinery — to the C. R. Daniels Company of Newark, New Jersey, for $65,000 at an auction was held in front of the general store to foreclose Gary & Sons's default under its mortgage. The company simply had been unable to survive the Depression.

A few years later, however, stimulated by the immense demand for canvas and denim during World War II, the factory again was humming. Operations continued until the floodwaters of tropical storm Agnes churned through the mill in 1972, but not before the Daniels Company itself, in a remarkable exercise of milltown proprietorship, had razed all the houses in 1968, destroying a town since named to the Register of Historic Places, evicting about a quarter of the mill's employees and many of its pensioners, but perhaps saving their lives and certainly their property from the subsequent devastation of Agnes.

Elysville got its start in the 1840's when the Elysville Manufacturing Company, consisting of Thomas Ely and his four brothers, started building the original stone mill, now roofless and gutted but with walls still standing. The Baltimore & Ohio Railroad already passed through the stretch of curving valley bottom. Constructing, equipping, and operating the mill were more costly than anticipated, and in 1845 the Ely brothers decided to convey it to a new corporation funded with more capital from additional shareholders. Accordingly, in 1846 the Elysville Company sold the mill to the newly-incorporated Okisko Company in exchange for $25,000 of Okisko stock. Five Baltimore merchants, who would soon wish they had never heard of Thomas Ely and his slippery brothers, paid another $25,000 for their shares in Okisko.

Further improvements were made, the fresh capital was spent, but still the enterprise floundered. In 1849 a suit was brought by unpaid contractors and other creditors demanding that the mill be sold to satisfy their claims. At this point the

Elysville Company brought its own suit asserting that the sale of the mill to Okisko was a nullity and urging that the mill, complete with $25,000 in additional improvements, be returned to the Elys or sold for their benefit on the grounds that the contract with Okisko had required that the Elysville Company be paid in cash and not stock, that Thomas Ely (as president of the Ely Corporation) had lacked power to sell the mill, and that the Elysville Corporation had been without charter authority to hold stock in another company such as Okisko. When the court attempted to sell the property, Hugh Ely, a state senator who was one of the brothers, bought the mill at the auction but then repudiated his purchase on the ground that the advertisement describing the property, which was based on an inventory that the Ely brothers themselves had prepared when selling the mill to Okisko, was inaccurate and misleading. Hugh Ely also testified in the principal case, but in its opinion the Court pointedly concluded that his testimony was utterly beyond credence. The intertwined litigation dragged on until 1853, reaching the state's highest court three times. Finally the property was sold for the benefit of creditors.

During the 1850's the mill was bought and sold by a succession of corporations, some of them simply reorganizations of prior owners. For a period the property was owned by the Alberton Manufacturing Company, one of whose principals was Jacob Albert, an Okisko creditor whose name stuck to the community. Late in the decade the mill and town came under the firm control of James S. Gary, a self-made man whose fortune propelled his son, James A. Gary, to the position of Postmaster General for President McKinley and to leadership of the Maryland Republican party until his death in 1920.

Under Gary ownership the mill at Alberton became a solid financial success for the first time, helped by large contracts for tents during the Civil War. In 1860 the mill employed 50 men and 120 women and owned 120 looms and 3,000 spindles. An oakum factory was also in operation making caulking from cotton waste. By 1895 the mill had grown to 340 looms, presumably run by an equal number of women and children, for

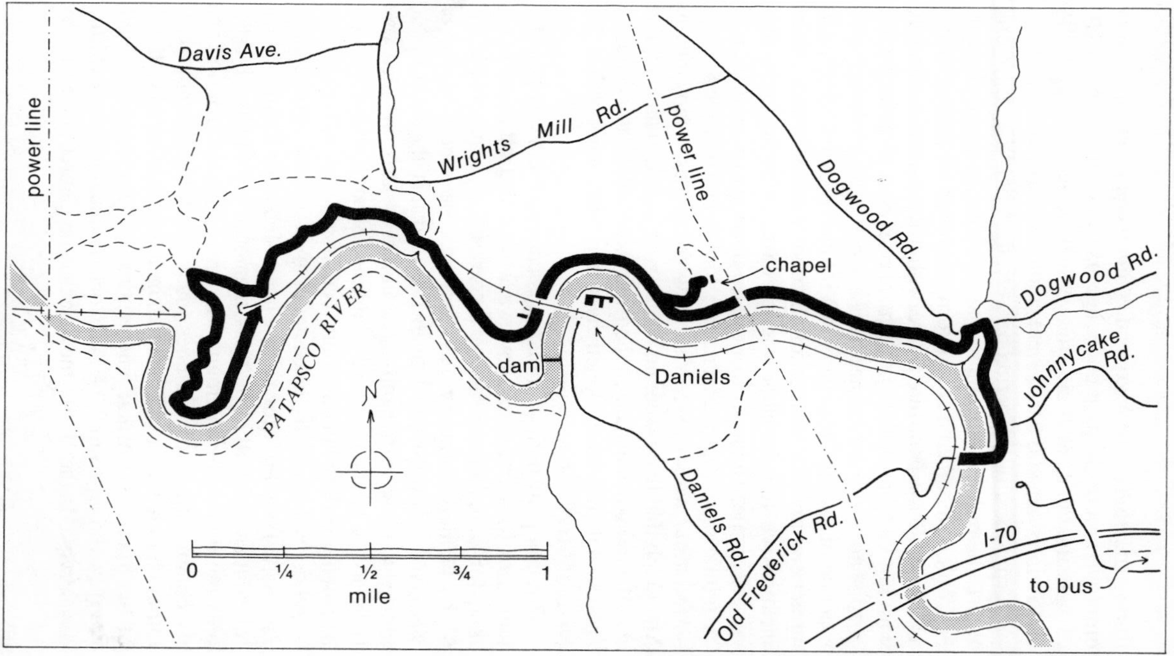

USGS: *Ellicott City*

during the 1890's the Maryland cotton manufacturing industry employed more children under age sixteen than any other type of manufacturer, with an average starting age of twelve. By 1915 more than 400 hands were employed at Alberton.

During most of the period between the Civil War and World War I, the mill and surrounding town were managed by Samuel F. Cobb, remembered by his former workers and subordinates as an Old Testament-like figure with a long white beard who was not only boss but *de facto* mayor as well, summoning outside authority only as need arose. Cobb's diaries describe the practice of sending recruiters to Virginia and West Virginia to attract employees — especially families with many girls, since inexpensive female labor was preferred. One recruiter purportedly enticed a family to move to Alberton to work in the mill by telling them that bananas, free for the picking, grew in the surrounding woods. When the new employees complained to Mr. Cobb that there were no bananas, he is said to have replied that the monkeys had eaten them all. Although almost certainly apocryphal, the story nonetheless may accurately reflect the tenor of Mr. Cobb's regime.

The company policy for management of the mill was a combination of long hours and low wages matched by equally low rents for large and comfortable houses. Even as late as 1968 the C. R. Daniels Company was charging a top rent of $4.50 per week for a seven-room house, provided that the head of the family worked in the mill. The company also provided free firewood, Christmas gifts for children, a school, and support for a growing variety of community activities.

Aside from the mill, the center of town life was the churches. James A. Gary built the Gary United Methodist Church on the hill south of the mill in 1879 as a memorial to his father. It is the only building in the community undamaged by flood or fire, and its congregation still includes many former mill employees. Other churches were encouraged, including the Catholic church of St. Stanislas Kostka, whose priest sometimes skated down the frozen river from the Woodstock Seminary to conduct Sunday service. In the 1920's the St. Stanislas Church was struck by lightning and burned. Its ruins are located on the hillside across the river and slightly downstream from the mill. An Episcopal congregation existed until World War I. Its stone church was later incorporated into the mill complex and is most easily seen from the side of the factory that is farthest downstream. In 1940 a small Pentecostal church was built near the railroad bridge across the river from the mill. At one point during the 1972 flood only the roof and tower of the church were visible. Dozens of company houses used to front the road above and below the church, which still stands today. The residents crossed to the mill on a pedestrian suspension bridge like the one at Orange Grove, discussed in Chapter 2.

Following World War I the company's business began to decline as the owners failed to modernize the mill. During the Depression operations nearly stopped altogether. Many employees worked only one or two days a week. Gary & Sons obtained a loan from the Reconstruction Finance Corporation, but when the firm was unable to keep up with the payments, the entire enterprise was sold to the C. R. Daniels Company. Daniels renovated the mill and fixed up much of the housing but eventually announced that it was going to demolish the dwellings because it could not afford the cost of still further repairs and improvements — estimated at $750,000 — in order to bring the residences up to housing code standards. Despite an outcry from local anti-poverty agencies and historic preservation groups, the town ceased to exist in 1968 although the mill continued in business.

In 1972 Agnes struck. The water rose so fast that five people were caught in the mill building and had to be evacuated from the roof by helicopter. The town store was pushed off its foundation and swept away. When the flood receded, cars, trucks, flotsam, and wreckage were left heaped against the buildings, which were coated inside and out with mud. Snarls of nylon yarn trailed from windows and the tops of telephone poles. The C. R. Daniels Company suffered an uninsured loss of $2.7 million and pulled out of the valley. The property passed through several hands, at one point selling for $25,000. Then in

1977 the mill, while being used as a warehouse, was gutted by fire. The brick portion of the mill has been repaired in part and as of 1980 was being used for the manufacture of roof trusses and other prefabricated construction items. The state has bought about 340 acres of the surrounding land for the Patapsco State Park, including land across the river from the mill where much of Elysville-Alberton-Daniels used to stand.

BUS: From downtown take the MTA Westview bus (#20) via Baltimore Street, Old Frederick Road, and Edmondson Avenue to the end of the line just beyond the Beltway (I-695). Get off at the corner of Chesworth Road and Denbright Road. You will know that your stop is coming after the bus crosses the Beltway and turns left off Crosby Road onto Chesworth Road.

From the bus stop a 3-mile walk is necessary to reach the beginning of the route outlined on the map. However, much of this additional mileage is itself along a pleasant path. Walk north on Chesworth Road to Crosby Road. Follow Crosby Road left (or west) past several intersections to Adamsview Road. Turn right on Adamsview Road and follow it straight and then to the left where it changes names to Johnnycake Road.

Continue on Johnnycake Road across Rolling Road. Just before an intersection with Apple Grove Court on the left, turn right off Johnnycake Road onto a dirt road and past a power line substation. Continue with the power line overhead and Route I-70 on your right. Eventually an asphalt park road and park facilities will appear on your left. Continue under the power line until it crosses the park road. Turn right on the park road over I-70. Follow the road downhill (past a spur road to the left) to the park entrance on Johnnycake Road. Turn left to the river's edge, where you join the route described below.

AUTOMOBILE: The walk starts where Old Frederick Road crosses the Patapsco River just north of Route I-70.

The bridge at Old Frederick Road can be reached from the east by following Security Boulevard to its end, then left on Greengage Road, right on Fairbrook Road, left on Johnny-cake Road, and left again at the river. From the west, the bridge can be reached from the Route 29 exit (Exit 85) off Route I-70. Follow Route 29 north. Turn right (east) on Route 99, then left on Old Frederick Road. Parking places are scarce but there are a number of spots in the vicinity of the Old Frederick Road bridge and along the river. More convenient parking is available on the road shoulder at the entrance to Alberton Road off of Dogwood Road, 0.4 mile upstream from the Old Frederick Road bridge, but there is room for only one or two cars.

The point where the Old Frederick Road crosses the Patapsco River was formerly Ellicotts Upper Mills, purchased by the Ellicott family in 1774 from James Hood, who in 1768 had built a dam and mill for grinding corn. Four years earlier the Ellicotts had bought undeveloped land farther downstream at what became the Lower Mills and later Ellicott City, as discussed in Chapter 3. At that time the Upper Mills was more valuable than the Lower Mills because it was located where the main road linking Baltimore and Frederick forded the river. When the Ellicott property was divided, the Upper Mills was assigned to Joseph Ellicott, the oldest of the three Ellicott brothers.

Joseph moved his family from Bucks County, Pennsylvania to the Upper Mills in 1775, when he was forty-four years old. He was already wealthy, having traveled to England ten years before to claim and liquidate his great-grandfather's estate to which he was heir. In Pennsylvania he had been high sheriff of Bucks County and a member of the provincial assembly. His preoccupation with mathematics, clockmaking, mill works, and mechanics had also earned him prominence in scientific circles, and it is said that as he got older, these interests almost completely precluded social intercourse even with his own family. One of his projects was a four-faced musical grandfather clock that played twenty-four tunes and marked seconds, minutes, hours, days, months and years, phases of the moon, and motions of the planets.

When Joseph moved to Maryland, he tore down the mill built by James Hood and constructed another for milling wheat using the latest inventions and improvements, many of his own design. On the shelf of land at the west end of the present bridge, he also built a large house and (on land later taken by the railroad) an ornamental garden with a fish pond and fountain spouting water ten feet high. When the Upper Mills tract was resurveyed in 1797, it was called "Fountainville."

Like his brothers at the Lower Mills, Joseph also built a general store that sold dry goods, silks, satins, and brocades, as well as the usual groceries. According to one account, ladies from Baltimore often took the trouble to ride out to the Upper Mills, and during the Revolution the store was frequented by French troops stationed in Baltimore. Nonetheless, society must have been limited. Four of Joseph's nine children married the orphaned brothers and sisters of the Evans family that the Ellicotts had brought with them from Pennsylvania.

Joseph died in 1780 but his widow, Judith, maintained her household at the Upper Mills until her death in 1809. By then the mill and store had greatly declined in value. The Frederick Turnpike had been relocated through the Lower Mills, which in time utterly eclipsed the small settlement farther upstream.

THE WALK: From the Old Frederick Road bridge over the Patapsco River, follow the road east over the river and then to the left upstream. Continue north along the river past the intersection with Johnnycake Road. Turn left at a "T" intersection with Dogwood Road and cross the bridge over Dogwood Run. Veer left onto Alberton Road immediately past the bridge. Alberton Road is closed to automobile traffic but open to pedestrian use.

Follow Alberton Road past a house and park gate. With the river on your left, continue upstream to Daniels, situated on the opposite bank.

St. Stanislaus Kostka Chapel

Where you first come opposite the ruins of Daniels, a road intersects from the right. This road leads uphill, through a park gate, and around the shoulder of a ravine to the left. The ruins of the old Catholic chapel of St. Stanislaus Kostka are located in the woods on the far side of the ravine shortly after the road bends left away from the river.

From the road opposite Daniels continue around the big bend in the river. After passing under the railroad tracks, veer left toward the dam where the main path climbs right toward the railroad. Continue on the less worn trail as it slowly curves right. Several paths lead left to the Daniels dam. Eventually the path will rejoin the river on the left, and then it joins the railroad tracks. Be alert for trains.

With the river on your left, follow the railbed a short distance to a bridge over a stream. Immediately after crossing the bridge, follow the path that climbs along the flank of the valley to the right of the railroad. Continue on this path as it bends in and out of several ravines. Rejoin the railroad just before a tunnel, but veer right immediately to follow the path uphill away from the railroad. When the path levels, turn left at a four-way trail junction. Follow the path up across the top of the hill through which the railroad tunnel passes. Continue as the path narrows and zigzags downhill to the river's edge. With the river on your right, follow the path downstream through the bottom of the curving valley until it gradually rises to join the railroad tracks near the mouth of the tunnel. Cross the tracks and rejoin the trail that you followed earlier back along the bluff to Daniels and your starting point near the Old Frederick Road bridge.

5

PATAPSCO VALLEY STATE PARK
McKeldin Recreation Area

Walking — 4 miles (6.4 kilometers). Well-marked, mostly level footpaths through the deep valleys and woods at the confluence of the South and North Branches of the Patapsco River. Not reachable by public transportation. The land along part of the South Branch is low, lush, and sunny; wildflowers crowd the bank. The North Branch is narrow, remote, wild, and in places lined with ferns and raspberries. A spur trail leads to McKeldin Falls, among the largest of our local cascades. Picnic facilities are available. During winter telephone beforehand in order to check whether the park is open on weekdays. Managed by the Maryland Park Service (747-6602).

"**F**RANKLY, I LIKE THE SOUND of the Governor Theodore R. McKeldin Recreation Area," said Governor Theodore R. McKeldin at the dedication ceremony for this section of the Patapsco Valley State Park in 1957. For more than a decade McKeldin had been one of the leading advocates for the expansion of the park to include the entire Patapsco Valley downstream from Sykesville as well as the North Branch below Liberty Reservoir. As governor, McKeldin was in the enviable position of being able to implement what he described as a "brilliant plan" for park expansion that he had come across after taking office — a plan developed earlier at his recommendation while mayor of Baltimore but shelved by the prior governor. The plan called for the extension into the greater Baltimore area of the system of stream valley parks first proposed in the Olmstead Brothers report fifty years earlier (discussed in Chapter 18).

Prior to the 1950's, the Patapsco Valley State Park included less that 1,500 acres in a patchwork between Route 40 (Hollofield) and Route 1 (Avalon). The park — or Patapsco Forest Reserve, as it was at first called — had started with a gift to the state of 43 acres in 1907, at a time when President Theodore Roosevelt (for whom McKeldin was named) and his chief forester, Gifford Pinchot, were popularizing the philosophy of conservation and adding millions of acres of land to federal ownership. In 1912 the state legislature for the first time appropriated funds for the purchase of forest lands to be managed by the Maryland State Board of Forestry. By the Depression, the Patapsco Forest Reserve included about 1,300 acres; during the next few years the area was improved with trails, picnic grounds, shelters, and campsites constructed by workers of the federally sponsored Civilian Conservation Corps. As the primary use of the area shifted from forest preservation to recreation, the name was changed to the Patapsco Valley State Park under the newly consolidated Department of State Forests and Parks.

In 1946 the Patapsco River Valley Commission, appointed by then-Mayor McKeldin, drew up a plan for enlarging the state park to 15,000 acres connected by a riverside parkway. The road was never built but other aspects of the plan reappeared in a study prepared by private consultants for the Maryland State Planning Commission in 1950. The new plan called for a linear park of 8,500 acres averaging half a mile in width and extending thirty-seven miles along the river from the Hanover Street Bridge to Sykesville. Improvements were to include not only the usual hiking and riding trails and picnicking and camping

facilities but also golf courses (even miniature golf), swimming pools, a miniature railroad, a carrousel, dance pavilions, restaurants, cabins, and lodges. The total cost was estimated at $6 million and a period of twelve years was thought sufficient to complete the project.

During the next twenty-five years the park grew in fits and starts. For a period land acquisition stalled at about 4,500 acres as funds were exhausted and state and local officials and a citizen advisory committee debated which land should be given priority for purchase. A major area of contention was the marsh along the lower Patapsco, where gravel mining had left a series of small lakes in the flats beside the river. This area has since been acquired at the urging of officials of Anne Arundel County and, although not yet developed for recreation, it promises to be one of the most unusual and interesting sections of the park. By 1972, when much of the Patapsco Valley was devastated by tropical storm Agnes, the park included about 7,000 acres spread among Baltimore, Howard, Carroll, and Anne Arundel Counties and was visited yearly by an estimated 4.5 million people.

Yet at the same time that millions of dollars were being spent to expand the park, industrial pollution and suburban growth were turning the Patapsco River into a regional sewer. At first the problem was not without drollery. Children who swam at Ellicott City in the early 1900's had to post a lookout on the rocks upstream to warn the others to get out of the water when the Dickey Mill at Oella released its dye into the river. But by mid-century swimming was unthinkable. Sykesville, Ellicott City, and other communities and institutional facilities dumped their untreated waste into the river. Newspaper accounts during the 1960's reported floating islands of bubbling sludge and a river bottom coated with decomposing matter. Massive fish kills occurred annually during periods of particularly toxic discharges. By 1967 a study by the Maryland Department of Water Resources classified the Patapsco River below Ilchester as "grossly polluted."

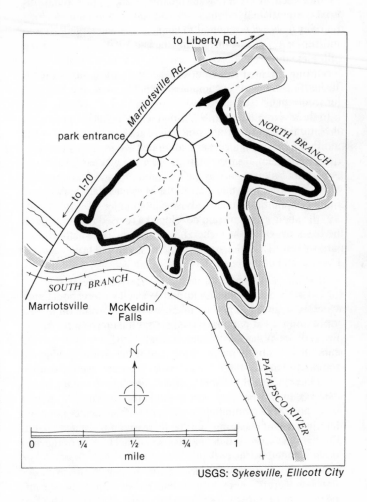

to Liberty Rd.

Marriotsville Rd.

park entrance

NORTH BRANCH

to I-70

SOUTH BRANCH

Marriotsville

McKeldin Falls

PATAPSCO RIVER

N

| 0 | ¼ | ½ | ¾ | 1 |

mile

USGS: *Sykesville, Ellicott City*

Since then, however, water quality in the Patapsco has improved significantly. Industries and most communities along the river have been required to connect into the large Patapsco interceptor sewer line that during the late 1960's was run up the valley from the Patapsco Wastewater Treatment Plant at Wagners Point. Also, the torrent caused by tropical storm Agnes flushed a century of accumulated filth from the riverbed (and dumped it in Chesapeake Bay).

In the aftermath of the 1972 flood, the Maryland Department of Natural Resources (into which the old Department of Forests and Parks had been incorporated) undertook to re-evaluate previous park plans for the Patapsco. The job was assigned to the Department's own staff in the Division of Land Planning Services. Working with members of the Maryland Park Service and a newly-appointed citizen advisory committee of sixteen people, the state's design team developed a revised master plan on the basis of which the General Assembly in 1980 authorized a park totaling 15,200 acres, of which 11,442 had been acquired as of the end of the year.

In 1980 the Patapsco project also received federal approval for assistance from the Land and Water Conservation Fund, which is financed in part by revenues from offshore oil leases, admission fees at national parks, taxes on motorboat fuels, and proceeds from the sale of surplus land. Under this program the state hopes to be reimbursed for half of the cost of buying the remaining land for the Patapsco park. The state share will come (as it has since 1969) from Program Open Space, funded by the state tax of 0.5 percent on real estate transactions. No matter what the source of funding, however, park advocates point out that the pace of spending must be increased if the state hopes to win the race with land developers and to acquire all of the area recommended by the park planners.

Aside from calling for a larger park, the new Patapsco master plan is generally more austere than earlier plans. The Department of Natural Resources has adopted the policy that the chief purpose of state parks is to promote the enjoyment and protection of natural, historic, and scenic features rather than to provide tennis courts, swimming pools, golf courses, and other recreation facilities that are the responsiblity of local governments (although the Patapsco plan still entails acquisition of an existing golf course and several pools).

Finally, the park will be expanded beyond the immediate valley. Previously the state had concentrated on buying only the valley bottom and slopes because they were visually and environmentally sensitive — and in most cases cheap as well. The new proposal calls for development of extensive campgrounds and picnic areas set back from the valley rim in areas that are beyond the reach of floods, easily accessible from nearby roads, and yet visually isolated in the woods. The valley slopes and bottomland will be reserved for low-cost improvements and low-key uses, such as riding and walking trails. The Park Service also hopes to build a nature interpretation center in the McKeldin Recreation Area and a history center off Frederick Road east of Ellicott City.

BUS: None.

AUTOMOBILE: The McKeldin Recreation Area of the Patapsco Valley State Park is located on Marriotsville Road south of Liberty Reservoir between the North and South Branches of the Patapsco River. From the intersection of Liberty Road and Marriotsville Road, the park entrance is 4.7 miles west on Marriotsville Road. From Exit 18 off Route I-70, the park entrance is 4.5 miles north on Marriotsville Road. On weekends and holidays during April through September, there is an entrance fee of $3 per car (as of 1981).

THE WALK: From the parking area and ranger station at the top of the entrance drive, follow the entrance road back downhill toward Marriotsville Road for 70 yards. At the first bend, veer left off the road onto the wide path entering the woods. This path is called the Switchback Trail and is marked with yellow blazes. Except for one stretch noted below, the route described here follows this trail in its entirety. White triangular markers occasionally point to trails that return to the central parking area.

Follow the path through the woods, then down and around to the left by Marriotsville Road. Continue along the bottom of the slope. At the next trail junction the white and yellow blazes indicate a path leading uphill to the left, but unless the water is too high or you wish to maximize the length of your walk, continue straight to the river's edge. You will rejoin the yellow-blazed trail later.

Turn left along the valley bottom. Eventually turn right at a "T" intersection where you rejoin the blazed trail. Follow the path uphill along the river bank, across an asphalt road, and down again to the river. At this point, a spur trail along the river's edge leads several hundred yards upstream and around the bend to McKeldin Falls.

With the river on your right, follow the path downstream to a large ledge sloping into the river. If you prefer not to cross the ledge, retrace your steps a few dozen yards and detour up and around the ledge and back down to the path by the river. Follow the path downstream to the confluence of the North and South Branches of the Patapsco.

With the river on the right, follow the North Branch upstream. After about three-quarters of a mile, fork right and follow the path along the valley bottom, around to the left, and along the river. Eventually you will pass a jumble of boulders shortly before the river bends slightly to the right, followed by more boulders in 100 yards. After another 120 yards, turn right to climb steeply away from the river. If you run into a cliff blocking further progress along the river's edge, you will know that you have gone too far and should retrace your steps 70 yards.

Follow the footpath as it climbs away from the water and turns right along the flank of the valley. Turn left at a "T" intersection. Follow the path to a picnic area and then an asphalt road that at one point provides a view of Liberty Dam to the north. Continue straight to the parking lot.

6

SOLDIERS DELIGHT

*Walking and ski touring — 3 to 5 miles (4.8 to 8 kilometers)
depending on whether you continue west of Deer Park Road. A
network of wide trails through rocky meadows and dry, stunted
woods. The unusual landscape and mineral soil makes Soldiers
Delight a botanist's delight. A wide variety of wildflowers,
grasses, sedges, mosses, and lichens may be seen here. However, avoid the mud season during spring thaw. Managed by the
Maryland Park Service (922-3044).*

THERE'S CHROME IN THEM THAR HILLS at Soldiers
Delight.

Perhaps this news lacks the galvanic impact of a gold strike,
but the fact remains that during the second quarter of the 19th
century, ownership of chromite mines in the Soldiers Delight
district northwest of Baltimore and at other outcroppings of
serpentine rock in Maryland and southeastern Pennsylvania
enabled Isaac Tyson, Jr., founder of the Baltimore Chrome
Works, to control the world chromium market and become a
very wealthy man.

The serpentine formations that break the surface in a few
locations north and west of Baltimore are like nothing else in the

region. They are commonly called serpentine *barrens*, and appropriately so. Blackjack oak, post oak, and Virginia pine (all small, drought-tolerant species) grow from the meager soil. Scattered through the woods are meadows of yellow grass. The faded colors and stunted forest offer hikers a refreshing change from the deep-soiled farmland, river gorges, and tall deciduous woods so typical of Maryland's Piedmont region. Birdwatchers will be disappointed with the dearth of species, but botanists can roll and revel in the Indian grass, beard grass, turkeyfoot and broom sedge. Depending on the season, visitors can also find bird's-foot violets, blazing stars, sundrops, Belgian asters, knotweed, goldenrod, fringed gentian, and many other flowers.

Serpentine is a greenish metamorphic mineral found near Baltimore not only in the Soldiers Delight region but also in the Bare Hills west of Lake Roland. At Cardiff in Harford County, serpentine is quarried and sold under the trade name of Maryland Green Marble, although it is not a limestone, as are true marbles. The rock is used primarily for interior trim in banks, hotels, and office buildings (including the lobby of the Empire State Building). Serpentine also has been tried as a structural building stone, despite the tendency of the rock surface to flake off due to weathering. The exterior of the Mt. Vernon Place Methodist Church, which has a distinctly greenish hue, is built of local serpentine.

More significantly, the occurrence of serpentine in Maryland is associated with the presence of chromium. In 1808 or 1810 chromium ore was discovered in the serpentine outcroppings at the Bare Hills estate of Jesse Tyson, a wealthy flour and grain merchant. The Tysons' gardener showed some black rocks to Tyson's son, Isaac, who was a student of geology, minerology, and chemisty. He identified the rocks as chromite, and analysis established that the ore was of a grade that was salable.

With financial assistance from his father, the young Tyson started mining the ore on a small scale. Ore was extracted at the Bare Hills as early as 1811, and by 1817 Tyson was also mining chromite from stream deposits (called placers) in the serpentine barrens at Soldiers Delight. As with gold mining, the stream

USGS: Reisterstown

sands were washed in a sluice (called a buddle) to concentrate the heavy chromite. The ore was then shipped to paint factories in England, for at that time chromium was used primarily to make brilliant pigments and dyes (hence chrome-yellow, chrome-orange, chrome-green, and other chrome hues).

Chromite mining was only a small part of Tyson's business as a manufacturer of chemicals and medicines, but in 1827 he hit pay dirt. He noticed that a cider barrel that had been brought in a wagon to Belair Market in Baltimore was steadied by rocks that he recognized as chromite. He traced the stone to the Reed farm near Jarretsville in Hartford County, obtained mineral rights to the property, and there, at what came to be called Chrome Hill, found a massive deposit of ore only eight feet below the surface. The Reed Mine was developed quickly and became so profitable that Tyson temporarily suspended his operations at other sites.

Tyson continued, however, to search out serpentine formations in Maryland and Pennsylvania, and he bought or leased property wherever there were indications of chromium. Not long after the Reed discovery, Tyson opened the Wood Mine in the State Line District of Lancaster County, Pennsylvania. This operation was another bonanza, eventually proving to be the richest chromium mine in the United States. Isaac Tyson's mines were far more productive and economical than other sources, with the result that between 1828 and 1850 virtually all of the chromium used in the world came from his mines.

Tyson's search for chromite also led to his involvement in the mining and smelting of iron and copper. In league with his partners, he eventually owned most of the copper deposits in Maryland. He visited pits, smelting plants, and iron works up and down the East Coast. He was a leader in the use of new and more efficient methods of refining ore, such as smelting with hard coal and pre-heating air to create a hot blast. Engrossed with mining and minerals, he or his agents investigated deposits and mining claims from Maine to Virginia, west to Arkansas and Missouri, and even in Cuba and Spain. "I am now going to Stafford in Vermont and for what purpose?" he wrote in his journal on December 1, 1833:

SOLDIERS DELIGHT

> All for the sake of gain and how great the sacrifice. My
> beloved wife not yet out of her bed and requiring the sympathy
> and solace of her husband. My little children requiring the care
> and attention of their father & my business neglected.... I am
> able to talk philosophically on these subjects and show the
> unreasonableness of avarice and the folly of accumulating wealth
> for children and yet I find myself pursuing the beaten track.

In 1845 Tyson and his associates established the Baltimore
Chrome Works for the manufacture of chromium compounds
from raw ore. The plant was located on Block Street at the
entrance to the Inner Harbor. Tyson's timing in this venture was
fortunate because the export market for unprocessed ore began
to decline after the discovery in 1848 of high-grade chromite in
Turkey by a geologist who had gained some of his experience
working for Tyson. Although the export of chrome ore from the
United States had practically ceased by 1860, the manufacture
of chromium compounds continued to prosper and was carried
on by Tyson's sons after his death in 1861.

Today the former Baltimore Chrome Works is part of the
Allied Chemical Corporation, and the old Block Street facility
south of Little Italy has become one of the largest chromium
processing plants in the world. The Tyson chromite mines,
however, have long since been exhausted, as have other deposits in the United States, including those in California that
were operated by Tyson's successors after the East Coast mines
were closed.

Tyson's principal operation at Soldiers Delight was the
Choate Mine. It was opened before 1839 and was worked
intermittently until about 1886. It consisted of an inclined shaft
sloping to the southwest for as much as 200 feet and fanning out
to a mine face 160 feet wide. During the chromium shortage
caused by World War I, when the mineral was needed for
high-grade steel, the Choate Mine was reopened for a brief
period, but was again closed with the signing of the armistice.
Using gasoline pumps, an attempt was made to rid the mine of
water in the late 1920's but ended when several men were

asphyxiated. The mine entrance is still visible but the sloping shaft should not be entered.

BUS: From the Greyhound Terminal at the intersection of Center and Howard Streets, take Rohrbaugh's Gettysburg bus northwest on Liberty Road to Harrisonville. Tell the driver that you want to get off at the intersection of Liberty Road and Deer Park Road by the Deer Park Shopping Center and that you will be returning from the same point later in the day. You will know that your stop is coming as the bus approaches a large water tower at the intersection with Deer Park Road. For the return trip be sure that you know the time of arrival for the bus that you plan to take and that you flag the bus as it approaches. Call 239-8000 for detailed schedule information.

Alternatively, the MTA Carriage Hill bus (# 28) runs northwest on Liberty Road to within a mile of Deer Park Road. Get off at the end of the line at the corner of Liberty Road and Pikeswood Drive.

From the intersection of Liberty Road and Deer Park Road, follow Deer Park Road north 2.3 miles to the parking area on the west side of the road in the middle of the reservation.

The walk outlined on the map can be reached in less distance by following Deer Park Road north to Dolfield Road. Turn east on Dolfield Road and follow it 0.5 mile to where the trail enters the woods on the left by a culvert under the road. Follow the trail into the woods and pick up the orange-blazed trail leading left.

AUTOMOBILE: The parking area for Soldiers Delight Natural Environment Area is located on the west side of Deer Park Road 2.3 miles north of the intersection with Liberty Road (Route 26). This intersection is about 5 miles northwest of Beltway Exit 18 and is marked by a large water tower.

SOLDIERS DELIGHT

THE WALK: As of 1981 the route described here was marked by orange blazes. Start at the parking area on the west side of Deer Park Road near the top of Berry Hill, where in 1853 John Berry was gibbeted for the murder of his mother and attempted murder of his father. From the south end of the parking area, cross the road and follow it south 60 yards to where the trail veers left into the woods. Turn left at the first fork, and then left again in 40 yards near the entrance to Isaac Tyson's Choate Mine. Continue past a trail leading left. At a "T" intersection turn right for 15 yards and then left on a trail that eventually narrows to a footpath. Notice the change in vegetation as you head into an area of deeper soil.

Turn right on a narrow footpath at a four-way trail intersection and follow the path through the woods to a large field with a house on the right.

Head straight across the clearing and driveway and re-enter the woods. Continue past a small pond about 20 yards to the right. Cross another clearing. Continue gently downhill to a "T" intersection near Dolfield Road. Turn right and follow the path through the woods, across a stream, and up a gentle slope through several clearings. Eventually, at a four-way trail intersection, you will cross the trail that you followed earlier.

Continue straight through the woods and through another clearing. Fork right at a trail junction. Follow the path down a gentle slope through more open spaces, past a trail intersecting from the right, and back into the woods. Turn left uphill through more clearings, left again at the next trail junction, and then right. Follow the path back to Deer Park Road, with the parking area to the left as you emerge from the woods.

If you want to extend your walk, another trail about two miles long and marked by green blazes forms a circuit on the west side of Deer Park Road. From the south end of the parking area, follow the road south 50 yards to where the

footpath veers half-right into the woods. Continue on the
footpath several hundred yards as it runs parallel to the
road before turning right on a gravel road. Follow this
road through a picnic area and to the left past Red Dog
Lodge. Fork left where the road splits in front of a large
field. Follow the road by a log cabin and then straight
toward a power line. Pass a dirt road intersecting from the
right. Turn right on a rutted road directly under the power
line and follow it downhill and then back to the crest of the
hill below the stone lodge passed earlier. Continue on the
power line trail to the bottom of the hill, but then turn right
to follow a footpath along a brook (upstream). Continue on
the footpath as it eventually veers up to the left away from
the stream and climbs to Deer Park Road, with the parking
area to the right as you leave the woods.

Soldiers Delight is a state "natural environment area," meaning that aside from trails no recreational development is planned.
The state first began to purchase land here in 1970 after ten years
of lobbying and fund raising by local conservation groups,
including the Citizens Committee for Soldiers Delight and
Soldiers Delight Conservation, Inc. Money has been supplied
by private donations and the county, state, and federal governments. About 1,500 acres had been purchased as of 1980, and
acquisition of an additional 500 acres is planned.

In case you have been wondering, there are at least half a
dozen explanations for the name "Soldiers Delight." The most
plausible relates not to troops but to the corruption of "Sollers,"
purportedly the name of an early German settler in the region.
But if you prefer, you can believe the one about the young ladies
who used to bring ice cream to soldiers who bivouacked in the
area while patrolling for Indians.

Cow-Parsnip, Heracleum maximum

7

OREGON RIDGE

Walking and ski touring — 4 miles (6.4 kilometers). From Oregon Lodge and ski slope straight to the crest of the ridge, then south through mature upland woods to Baisman Run and Ivy Hill Pond. Return on a pleasant loop past Oregon Lake, where supervised swimming is permitted during the summer. The path is broad, easy, and blazed with red markers. Managed by the Baltimore County Department of Recreation and Parks (666-8966).

THE VIEW FROM OREGON RIDGE looks north over the agricultural valleys of Oregon Branch and Western Run. To the northwest is Hayfields, long the estate of the Bosley and Merryman families, where in 1824 the Marquis de Lafayette visited Colonel Nicholas Merryman Bosley and presented him with a silver trophy from the Maryland Agricultural Society for superior cultivation of the land. Immediately to the east is the Hunt Valley Business Community, since 1962 a major new source of nonagricultural employment. Farther north is Loveton Center, another new industrial complex (visible in the right-center of the photograph). Just beyond the fields in the center of the picture is Interstate 83, putting this attractive farm landscape within a half hour's drive of downtown Baltimore. Not surprisingly, in more than a few places during recent years the fields of corn, barley, and soybeans have been replaced by scattered new houses and subdivisions. In fact, Hayfields itself is now owned

View from Oregon Ridge

by Hayfields, Inc., which has been exploring different proposals for residential development of its 474-acre farm.

This setting and its obvious development potential epitomize areas that are the subject of growing national concern about the loss of farmland. The concern is both aesthetic and economic. The conversion of farmland to scattered, low-density subdivisions (by far the most voracious use of land) not only chews up the countryside but also imposes on local governments an obligation to develop public services and capital improvements that typically cost much more than similar improvements for high-density housing — and more, too, than is generated in new tax revenues. Also, land that is easily developed for residential use because of level, deep, well-drained soils is for the same reasons excellent for crops. According to a Congressional report released in 1978, about one third of the three million acres of farm and pasture that is developed each year in the United States is prime agricultural land capable of feeding at least 2.9 million people annually but which never again will be used for producing food.

The rapid growth of suburban Baltimore, Washington, and other cities and towns has made Maryland a national leader in farmland loss, although not all of the decline is attributable to land development. When the suburban explosion began at the end of World War II, Maryland farms accounted for 4.2 million acres, or 67 percent of the state's total land. By 1980 farm acreage had dwindled to about 2.4 million acres, or 38 percent of the state's land area. By the year 2000 Maryland is expected to lose an additional 1 million acres of farmland, and all Marylanders presumably will pay the added transportation costs of importing still more produce from other states and other countries.

Faced with the steady transformation of farms into suburbia, Maryland has developed a variety of programs intended to encourage the continued use of land for farming. In 1956 Maryland was the first state to enact a law (now Article 81, § 19 of the Annotated Code of Maryland) requiring that farmland be assessed for property taxes not on the basis of its full development value

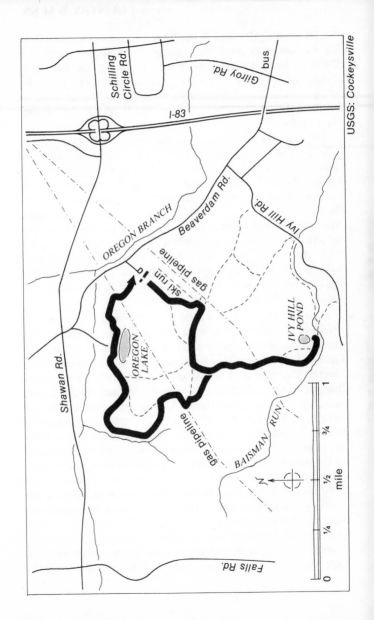

USGS: Cockeysville

but rather on the basis of its use for farming, as though that were all the land was good for. This preferential assessment was intended to provide staying power to farmers on the urban fringe, where higher taxes based on the land's enormous development potential supposedly were forcing farmers out of business (that is, causing them to sell their land for very substantial profits).

The remarkable thing about the preferential tax program, which with a few modifications has weathered a series of stormy attacks, is that landowners are required to give almost nothing in return. At most an owner who develops his farm property is simply required to pay a development tax equal to 10 percent of the difference between the land's agricultural assessment and its full development value. Thus in Baltimore County, where the tax rate in 1980 was 3.13 percent, the development tax equals about three years' worth of the taxes that would have been paid anyway but for the preferential assessment. If the owner holds the land for more than three years he has saved taxes and is still free to sell his land whenever he wants.

Equally remarkable is that despite the annual revenue loss of millions of dollars to the state and county treasuries, no evidence exists that the preferential assessment helps to preserve farmland. *Untaxing Open Space,* a 1976 report prepared for the federal government's Council on Environmental Quality, found that preferential assessment of agricultural land probably deters only one percent of all farmers from selling their land for development. Dr. Sidney Ishee of the University of Maryland, a longtime student of differential assessment in the state, speculates that the law's principal effect is a temporary postponement of the development of farmland in some instances, but that the tax benefits are simply not strong enough to deter farmers near Baltimore and Washington from selling out at prices which in 1976 ranged up to ten times the farm use value of the land and have since gone higher.

Some land experts even argue that the preferential farm assessment encourages suburban sprawl. The artificially low taxes on farmland near cities enable owners to hold land off the market while prices climb higher still, with the result that development leapfrogs farther out. Even if preferential assessment does not encourage inefficient patterns of land development, there is little doubt that the tax break simply subsidizes speculators by reducing their holding costs, since any land that is farmed, regardless of ownership, qualifies for lower taxes. Land that has been sold to real estate syndicates at prices reflecting full development value continues to be assessed as though it were fit only for farming. For example, Hayfields, bought by Hayfields, Inc. in 1978 for $2,200,000, was assessed in 1980 at $171,150.

Recognizing the ineffectiveness of preferential assessment to prevent the loss of farmland over the long term, the Maryland General Assembly has embarked on other efforts to obtain a more binding preservation commitment from farm owners. Of course, the usual way to gain permanent control over land is to buy it. But it is not necessary to buy the full interest in land — the so-called fee interest. Instead the state proposes to buy easements restricting development of the land. The term "easement" is somewhat misleading because these development right easements are *negative,* entailing nothing more than the extinguishment of the owner's right to develop his farmland to a more intensive use. The public is not granted the right of access, as with an *affirmative* easement. Nor does purchase of the development rights enable the state to develop the land; it merely gives the state the enforceable right to prevent the landowner from doing so. And because the owner retains the right to farm his land just as he always has, acquisition of the development rights does not cost as much as purchase of the fee interest.

The preservation of farmland through the purchase of development right easements is one of the chief functions of the Maryland Agricultural Land Preservation Foundation, which was established in 1977 as an agency of the Maryland Department of Agriculture. As spelled out in §§2—501 through 2–515 of the Maryland Agricultural Code Annotated, the acquisition process begins with the filing of a petition by landowners to establish an agricultural preservation district. If the petition is approved by the local government and the Agricultural Land Preservation Foundation, landowners within the district must agree to maintain their land in agricultural use for at least five years. In return the local government must adopt an ordinance permitting and promoting agricultural activities within the district in order to protect farmers from nuisance suits and restrictive legislation filed by suburbanites who, for all their talk of the joys of country life, frequently are annoyed by the normal smells, sounds, and dust of farm operations. This protection for normal agricultural use is an important consideration in developing areas, where what some studies call an "impermanence syndrome" can develop among farmers who see land use patterns changing and farmers' political clout in local government weakened.

Once farmland is located within a preservation district, its owners may sell easements disposing of their development rights to the Agricultural Land Preservation Foundation. If the sale is approved, the purchase price is set by law as the difference between the value of the land with and without the bar on development (unless the owner's asking price is lower). A deed containing convenants that restrict the farmland to agricultural use is recorded among the county land records. The convenants are perpetual, although an owner can apply to buy the development rights back after twenty-five years or sooner if profitable farming is no longer feasible. If the resale is approved, the landowner must pay the then-market value of the development rights.

Aside from receiving the purchase price, farmers who sell development right easements to the Foundation may realize other benefits also. For example, Article 81, §12E-1 of the Maryland Annotated Code provides that counties and cities may grant such owners a tax credit toward local school, special district, and general taxes. A substantial added incentive to sell development rights would exist were it not for the present state of the law: because the sale of development rights reduces the value of the land, the property tax assessment should be reduced correspondingly, yet preferential farm assessment already grants all farmers this favored treatment even though they retain development rights.

The principal impediment to Maryland's complex agricultural preservation program is lack of money. Alan Musselman, executive director of the program, estimates that the funding requirements for the acquisition of development rights will be between $10 and $15 million annually, with the eventual goal of preserving approximately two million acres of land at a total cost (at 1980 prices) of $2 billion. However, the actual funding granted the program during 1977-1981 was $5.7 million. Of this amount, all but $600,000 (which came from the farm development tax discussed earlier) was taken from the state's Program Open Space, ordinarily used for the purchase of recreational land, such as the underfunded Patapsco Valley and Gunpowder State parks, to which the public has the right of access. A number of counties, however, including most of those near Baltimore, have assisted the state's farm preservation program with matching funds of their own.

As of the end of 1980, more than 32,000 acres of farmland had been placed in agricultural districts under the preservation program, and easements restricting development had been acquired on twelve farms totaling 2,200 acres, mostly in the urban fringe of Anne Arundel, Baltimore, Carroll, Frederick, Harford, and Howard Counties. The easements cost about one third of the market value of the land. An additional seventy-eight farms containing 11,000 acres were under consideration at the outset of 1981.

Another state agency that is active in the preservation of farmland (as well as other undeveloped areas) is the Maryland Environmental Trust within the Department of Natural Resources. The Trust does not buy restrictive easements but merely acts as the recipient of donations by owners who share the Trust's goal of preserving scenic countryside and who welcome the substantial income tax deductions and estate tax savings that their donations produce. If the land has a substantial development potential, the charitable deduction resulting from a gift of the development rights to a governmental body can be very large. And once the owner conveys the development rights, the fair market value of the property for estate and property tax purposes drops correspondingly. Moreover, as in the case of easements given to the Agricultural Land Preservation Foundation, the counties are authorized to grant credits relating to various county and special district taxes on lands for which easements have been given to the Maryland Environmental Trust — but as of the end of 1980, only Montgomery and Prince Georges Counties had passed the necessary ordinance. At that time, the Trust held easements on fifty-six properties totaling 13,286 acres.

Because of the expense entailed in the purchase of development right easements and the understandable reluctance of most owners to give them away, some of the county governments are experimenting with a related approach designed to attract *private* money to the purchase of *transferable* development rights. In Calvert and Montgomery Counties, a landowner in an agricultural district can sell his development rights to a developer who holds land in certain other designated development zones. Purchase of added development rights enables the developer to build residential units on his own land — not the farmer's land — at a higher density than he would otherwise be permitted. This approach is supposed to help restrict farmland to farm use while at the same time promoting the more compact and efficient use of land in designated development zones, all at no cost to state or local governments.

Many counties are reluctant to rely upon voluntary programs entailing compensation to landowners in order to restrict the development of farmland. Instead, local zoning ordinances attempt to discourage development in such areas by requiring large residential lots and various other limitations. For example, most of rural Howard County is zoned for lots of at least three acres, and parts of other counties are subject to a minimum development density of ten, twenty, and twenty-five acres per lot. In the past, however, large lot zoning has proven ineffective in preventing conversion of farmland to residential use. In fact, large lot zoning simply squanders farmland by forcing develop-

ers to use more land for fewer houses, which are then touted as "estates" and "farmettes" on the subdivision signs.

Some counties have gone a step farther than conventional large lot zoning by establishing agricultural preservation zones where farming is promoted and other land uses are severely restricted. For example, the Baltimore County Agricultural Preservation zone limits residential development to a maximum density of two houses per hundred acres.

Finally, in addition to state and local governments, various private conservation groups are active in the preservation of agricultural land and other scenic areas. Many of these groups, including the nationally active Nature Conservancy, the Chesapeake Bay Foundation, and the Conservation Trust of the Greenspring and Worthington valleys, themselves acquire restrictive easements. The Valleys Planning Council is a local group active in the preservation of land in north-central Baltimore County, including the area in the vicinity of Oregon Ridge.

BUS: From downtown Baltimore take the MTA Hunt Valley bus (#9) via Charles Street and York Road through Towson to the Hunt Valley Business Community. Get off at the corner of Gilroy Road and Beaver Dam Road within the industrial park. You will know that your stop is coming after the bus turns right from Schilling Circle Road onto Gilroy Road.

From the bus stop walk west 1.5 miles on Beaver Dam Road over Interstate 83 to the entrance to Oregon Ridge Park.

AUTOMOBILE: The entrance to Oregon Ridge Park is on Beaver Dam Road 0.6 mile southeast of the intersection with Shawan Road. This intersection is one mile west of the Shawan Road exit (Exit 20B) off the Baltimore-Harrisburg Expressway (I-83).

OREGON RIDGE

THE WALK: From the parking area walk to the back of the lodges and enter the woods on a trail starting about 100 yards to the right of the ski slope. This trail is marked by red blazes, as is the entire walk described here.

Follow the trail uphill through the woods. Fork left and climb to the top of the ski slope. (If the Oregon Ridge concert pavilion is ever built, it may block the trail entrance; in that event, simply follow the ski run uphill.)

From the top of the ski run, follow the trail back away from the valley for 50 yards. Turn right at a "T" intersection. Follow the wide path through the woods past a trail intersecting from the right. At the next trail junction veer left. Continue past another trail intersecting from the right (you will take that path when you return from Ivy Hill Pond). Continue on the wide path through the woods across a gas pipeline right-of-way and down to the spillway from Ivy Hill Pond.

Return from the pond by the way you came. Several hundred yards after recrossing the pipeline clearing, fork left off the main path onto the trail that you passed earlier. At a "T" intersection turn left. Follow the path to another gas pipeline right-of-way. Turn right to follow the right-of-way 160 yards before veering left at the top of the hill to re-enter the woods on the far side of the pipeline clearing.

Fork left off the main path to follow the red blazes. Follow the path along the flank of a ravine and eventually uphill to the right. Continue straight where another path intersects from the right. Emerge from the woods at Oregon Lake, formed by a pit where iron ore was mined. Pass the beach and turn left immediately after a long bathhouse. Climb a low ridge and follow a rutted road to a field. Turn right along the edge of the field to return to the lodges and parking area.

8

GUNPOWDER FALLS STATE PARK

West Hereford

*Walking — 6.5 miles (10.5 kilometers). Well-marked footpaths
along the valley slopes, ridge tops, and river bank bordering
Big Gunpowder Falls. Follow the rocky gorge upstream to
Prettyboy Dam. Not reachable by public transportation. Picnic
facilities and youth group campsites are available near Bunker
Hill Road. During winter telephone beforehand in order to
make sure the park is open on weekdays. Managed by the
Maryland Park Service (592-2897).*

WHEN DOG BITES MAN, according to the old newspaper
adage, that's nothing, but when man bites dog, that's news. In
the same vein, we have grown accustomed to hearing of the
ongoing conflict between developers, loggers, and highway
planners on the one hand and nature lovers and environmentalists
on the other. Somewhat surprising, then, is the opposition by
some northern Baltimore County residents (whose avowed goal
is a viable park for their region) to the further development of the
Hereford section of the Gunpowder Falls State Park. Surprising,
that is, until we remember that to the residents of this area (many
of whom only recently fled the city) the state park conjures the
specter of more people — particularly people from Baltimore
with their blankets, beer, and barbecues.

Like the Patapsco River, long stretches of the Big and Little
Gunpowder Falls have been developed into a linear valley park.
Most of the park follows the Big Gunpowder Falls diagonally

across Baltimore County from northwest to southeast — from just below Prettyboy Reservoir to the river's mouth at Chesapeake Bay. Another arm follows the roughly parallel course of the Little Gunpowder Falls, which forms the boundary between Baltimore and Harford Counties.

Compared to Baltimore City's basic park system, which was created at about the turn of the century, the Gunpowder Falls State Park is relatively new, having been planned and acquired in response to the rapid suburbanization of Baltimore County after World War II. Since 1958, when the Maryland State Planning Commission first recommended a system of unconnected parks along both branches of the Gunpowder Falls, the Maryland General Assembly has authorized acquisition of 15,096 acres, of which more than 75 percent had been purchased by the end of 1980. Of course, some sections of the Big Gunpowder Falls already had been dammed and flooded to form Baltimore's reservoirs. Other parts of the two river valleys were excluded from the plan because they were thought to be unsuited for a park.

With the exception of the Hammerman area, which has swimming and picnicking facilities for thousands of people, most of the Gunpowder Falls State Park is undeveloped for uses other than hiking. A master development plan released in 1967 recommended an extensive system of playing fields, trails, bridges, campgrounds, picnic pavilions, and even cabins, swimming reservoirs, and a "frontier village" play center, but for the most part the plan has never been implemented. In 1977, when the Maryland Park Service tried to develop an equestrian center and a large complex of picnic pavilions and toilets for three thousand visitors at Bunker Hill Road in the heart of the Hereford section of the park, the residents of the area were so alarmed that they formed a group called the Northern Baltimore County Citizens Committee, which succeeded in having the funds for the project deleted from the state's budget.

There now appears to be a consensus among the state's planning officials, park users, and area residents that many of the facilities proposed in the 1967 master development plan

USGS: Hereford

parking
toilets
Bunker Hill Rd.
MINGO BRANCH
Bunker Hill Rd.
power line
FALLS
GUNPOWDER
BIG
MASEMORE Rd.
BUSH CABIN RUN
Prettyboy Dam
FALLS Rd.

N

0   ¼   ½   ¾   1
mile

were inappropriate for a state park. In a new preliminary concept plan that was prepared by the state's Division of Land Planning Services and released in 1978, the proposed use of the Bunker Hill area was scaled down drastically from the 1967 plan and the equestrian center moved to another location. Nonetheless, the new plan again was attacked vehemently by the Northern Baltimore County Citizens Committee, which claimed that the community had not been consulted adequately. In response Secretary James B. Coulter of the Department of Natural Resources suggested that the Northern Baltimore County group prepare its *own* development plan — the third such plan in a dozen years.

For the most part the controversy centered on adequate control and supervision of visitors to the park. Residents of the Hereford area were angered and appalled by vandalism and littering in the park. The covered bridge that once spanned the river at Bunker Hill Road had been burned, repaired, and burned again. On summer weekends roads approaching other bridges became clogged with parked cars. At some spots gatherings often continued into the night. Residents who complained of lack of policing by the Maryland Park Service were told that the most troublesome areas, although scheduled for acquisition, were still privately owned and thus beyond the control of the park rangers.

In the fall of 1979 the Northern Baltimore County Citizens Committee released its counter-plan. Surprisingly (after all the controversy) most of the local proposals were identical with those developed by the state's planners. An interpretive center for school field trips from throughout the region would be developed near the Hereford High School on York Road. Family picnicking and other activities would be centered in the area at the end of Bunker Hill Road. A parking lot for 125 cars would be built there and smaller lots constructed near the bridges farther upstream. All parking lots would be controlled by gates closed at night. Guardrails and boulders would discourage parking along roads. Illegally parked cars would be ticketed or even towed.

There were, however, differences between the state and local plans. A series of meetings over the course of yet another year was required to ponder, debate, and resolve such issues as whether a toilet should be built at each of the two parking lots upstream from Bunker Hill (suggested by the park planners but opposed by the community), whether small parking lots should be provided near bridges downstream from Bunker Hill (opposed by the community), and whether camping should be allowed at Bunker Hill (again opposed by residents of the area). A local bow-and-arrow club wanted an archery range, and joggers suggested that an exercise course be built. Owners on Bunker Hill Road wanted a new access road to bypass their houses, even though all of the properties were and are slated for acquisition. An entire meeting was devoted to canoeists and "tubers" — kids of all ages who float down the river in inner tubes. Local fishing groups, which by this time had joined the fray, wanted part of the river closed to boats. Even owners of streamside property below the park took the occasion to complain of canoeists and tubers trespassing on what they viewed as their river and wanted to know what the Department of Natural Resources was going to do about it.

Finally, there was much ado about picnicking: its proper place and practice. Picnickers — they are sometimes loud and sometimes litterers — are disliked by many residents living near the park, especially when on a club or church excursion the outsiders arrive *en masse* by charter bus or car caravan. Indeed, in the course of the controversy, *picnicker* became a term of aversion and scorn, comparable to *shoebee* on the New Jersey beaches (a nonresident who brings his lunch in a shoebox) or a *chickennecker* on the Eastern Shore (a city resident who crosses the Bay Bridge to catch crabs with chicken necks). As one Hereford resident wanted to know, "Why can't they go to places that are *closer*?"

Suffice it to say that after years of acrimony the park planners and community now appear to be in substantial agreement. Residents are particularly pleased by the increased ranger staff. As for physical improvements, under the present plan no group picnic pavilions will be developed in the Hereford section. Family picnicking and camping by supervised youth groups will be permitted at Bunker Hill, but nowhere else in the area. An archery range and jogging trail will be developed. Small parking lots will be provided at all bridges, but not toilets, at least for the time being. Canoers and tubers will be barred from prime fishing areas. Walkers, however, are welcome.

Another source of local ill will toward the state park has been the sometimes painful process of land acquisition. Although most owners, particularly owners of vacant land, have been amenable to selling, some unhappiness is inevitable when the state sets out to purchase about three dozen homes and more than 15,000 acres (4,000 acres in the Hereford area alone).

Price, of course, is the principal issue. To protect the interests of both the property owner and the state, the Department of General Services, which is the agency that handles land acquisition for Maryland's parks, is required to hire two independent appraisers to make separate determinations of fair market value of each property. The appraisals are reviewed by the Department's staff and if one or the other is approved, an offer in that amount is made to the owner. Sometimes a third apraisal is necessary if the first two figures are far apart, for the evaluation of real estate is not a precise technique. Occasionally an owner will obtain yet another appraisal of his own which may convince the state's reviewers and the Board of Public Works (which must approve all acquisitions) that a higher price is in fact justified.

If a price cannot be agreed upon, the Department of General Services in consultation with the Department of Natural Resources may simply wait in order to try again later with a new appraisal and offer. Or the matter may be turned over to the Attorney General's Office for condemnation, so that eventually the value of the property is decided by a jury unless the case is first settled by agreement. If the state declines to pay the amount set by the jury and instead abandons the acquisition, the owner's legal costs are paid by the state.

The procedural safeguards of appraisal and condemnation are

intended, of course, to provide a neutral determination of fair market value. For some properties, however, a price may be *fair* but nonetheless *inadequate*. For example, if forced to sell for fair market value, the owner of an unusually small or dilapidated or substandard house could not today buy another home in his community for what his own is worth. Until recently, the result of this dilemma was an impasse in the acquisition of some such properties for the Gunpowder Falls State Park. In 1979, however, when the Gunpowder project began to receive federal funds, the payment of relocation assistance became mandatory under federal law. As of 1980, payments of up to $15,000 (in addition to the agreed acquisition price) were authorized to help displaced homeowners to buy comparable houses nearby that are also "decent, safe and sanitary." In addition, state assistance of up to $500 has long been available to cover actual moving costs.

For some owners, however, the problem has not been price but preference: a simple desire to stay where they are. These cases have dragged on for years until only the most difficult are left, often involving holdings entirely surrounded by park property or wedges of private ownership penetrating deep into the park. Recently the Department of General Services has started to reach a variety of arrangements with people who do not want to move from their homes. Elderly owners commonly are offered a life license under which the state acquires the property outright for its full value while the former owners retain the privilege to occupy the house for the rest of their lives. They maintain and insure the property but pay no taxes or rent. Younger owners are sometimes offered a life estate, which requires that the purchase price be reduced by the value of the seller's right of continued occupancy, as estimated by their life expectancy. Also, owners of the life estate continue to pay property taxes. Finally, in some cases the state has bought the property and then leased it back to the former owners, an arrangement that has been popular with those who wish to avoid moving for a few years and also with farmers who are approaching retirement.

Around the perimeter of the park, the state has had trouble buying parts of individual holdings needed to form a readily identifiable boundary that bears an intelligent relationship to the topography of the area and to local streets. Owners have complained that their "back yards" are being taken — that is, tracts stretching hundreds of feet into the woods behind their houses. With these owners the Department of General Services is experimenting with a variety of affirmative and negative easements. The former allows certain public uses of the land and the latter prohibits development or logging. All of these techniques not only ease the acquisition process but also reduce the state's purchase expenses and maintenance costs.

BUS: None.

AUTOMOBILE: From the Mt. Carmel Road exit (Exit 27) off of the Baltimore-Harrisburg Expressway (I-83), turn east on Mt. Carmel Road and then left at a "T" intersection with York Road (Route 45). Soon after passing Hereford High School, turn left on Bunker Hill Road. Follow Bunker Hill Road to the large parking area.

THE WALK: Start at the field where Bunker Hill Road meets the river. A pedestrian bridge over the river is planned for this location. If it has been built, you may want to return at the end of your walk along the north bank of the river as noted below.

With the river on your right, climb half-left across the field. Twenty yards past a toilet house, turn sharp left on a grassy path. Follow the path sixty yards, then turn right on the Gunpowder South Trail (blue dots). The route described here follows the blue dot trail all the way to Prettyboy Dam.

Follow the blue dot footpath through some pines and downhill to the right. Cross a stream, turn left, and zigzag uphill and along the top of the bluff overlooking the river valley to the right. Pass a trail junction where the Mingo

Forks Trail (pink dots) intersects from the left. Continue straight downhill along a ravine to the edge of the Big Gunpowder Falls. With the river on your right, follow the path upstream to Masemore Road.

From the south end of the Masemore Road bridge, continue upstream with the river on your right. Fork right to continue along the river bank and across a small stream. Follow the riverside path upstream to Falls Road.

Cross Falls Road and continue upstream with the river on your right. Climb up to the left, then down again around a large rock formation. Give wide berth to any snakes sunning themselves on the rocks. Some people claim to have seen copperheads in this area. Eventually, as the river bends sharply left, the path becomes smoother. Then, as the river begins to turn right, fork left uphill along the side of the valley to the intersection with the Highland Trail (pink dots). You will take this trail on the return leg. For now, turn right downhill on the blue dot trail. Continue along the river's edge to the base of Prettyboy Dam. You can climb to the top of the dam on a trail starting by the river opposite a large flat rock about 200 yards below the dam.

Return downstream to the intersection with the High- land Trail that you passed earlier. Turn right and follow the pink dots uphill. Turn left at a "T" intersection and follow the ridge uphill to Falls Road. Cross Falls Road and continue on a road opposite. Fork left through green steel posts. (A parking lot may be built here and also a new trail leading downhill to the river.) Continue on the pink dot trail through the woods more or less parallel with the slope. Cross a power line right-of-way and re-enter the woods on a footpath marked by pink dots. Descend to a stream and follow it upstream. Cross the stream just before the path re-emerges at the power line right-of-way. Turn left and climb to an intersection with a wide path. Follow the path left until you rejoin the Gunpowder South Trail (blue dots) by the river's edge. Turn downstream to Mase-more Road.

If the pedestrian bridge at Bunker Hill has been built, cross the Masemore Road bridge and turn right down-stream on the riverside footpath leading to Bunker Hill. Otherwise, follow Masemore Road right sixty yards to pick up the blue dot trail where it crosses Bush Cabin Run on stepping stones a few yards downstream from the parking area guardrail. This is the trail which you took earlier from Bunker Hill. Follow it back to your starting point.

9

GUNPOWDER FALLS STATE PARK
East Hereford

Walking — 4 miles (6.4 kilometers). From York Road down-stream along a wild and winding stretch of river to Panther Branch. Return through woods and farmland above the valley. The footpaths are blazed with colored disks. Not reachable by public transportation. Managed by the Maryland Park Service (592-2897).

In COMMON PARLANCE in these parts, Baltimore is 'Bawlamer'. A brief lexicon of other Bawlamer locutions, such as 'Merlin' for Maryland, 'Naplis' for our state capital, 'Anna Runnel' and 'Harrid' for two of our nearby counties, and 'Droodle' for Druid Hill, is contained in the urban guidebook *Bawlamer,* published by the Citizens Housing and Planning Association. Less well-known, however, is that our Baltimore dialect is marked by other geographic expressions that are peculiar not for pronunciation but for usage.

Heading the list is *falls,* as in the Big Gunpowder Falls. The focus of the present chapter, of course, is not a local Niagara or even a waterfall at all. Indeed, during dry periods or at other times when water is not being released from Prettyboy Reservoir or Loch Raven, the Gunpowder not only does not *fall* but scarcely even *flows*.

According to William B. Mayre, a Maryland historian who made a specialty of place names, court records, and old documents of every variety, Baltimore County and its environs are

the only area in the United States where there are whole fresh-water rivers and streams called *falls*. Apparently early settlers along the tidal shores of the Gunpowder River and the Patapsco River (or rather 'Patapsico', in our local patois) called the swift and rocky freshwater streams above tidewater the *falls* of those rivers. Hence Big Gunpowder Falls and, for the smaller stream to the north, Little Gunpowder Falls, both emptying into the tidal Gunpowder River. Jones Falls is the freshwater portion of the Northwest Branch of the Patapsco River. Gwynns Falls is the falls of the Middle Branch. Similarly, old maps and other documents call the main branch of the Patapsco that flows through the state park Patapsco *Falls*. An early 19th-century print on display at the Maryland Historical Society depicts the original mill at Oella and states on its face: "Union Manu-factories of Maryland on Patapsco Falls, Baltimore County."

If a major freshwater stream of the Baltimore Piedmont is a *falls*, a middling stream is a *run* and a minor one a *branch*. Hence in Baltimore we have Dead Run, Western Run, Stony Run, Chinquapin Run, Herring Run, and Moores Run. As noted in the last chapter, two of the tributary runs and branches feeding the Big Gunpowder Falls are Bush Cabin Run and Mingo Branch, and the present walk passes Panther Branch.

With the exception of the various tidal arms of Baltimore Harbor, the saltwater counterpart to a tributary run or branch is a *creek*, unless the saltwater appendage is so small and serpentine as to be a *gut*. Thus, off the north side of the Patapsco River we have in rapid succession North Point Creek, Shallow Creek, Bear Creek, and Colgate Creek. In the Baltimore region there are only a few exceptions (notably Deer Creek) to the reserva-tion of *creek* for a small tidal river. And off the creeks branch myriad *coves*.

Finally, perhaps you are wondering about *brook*. Mr. Mayre dismisses the term as "literary." It is virtually never seen in old deeds or other documents and appears only in the contrived names given to housing subdivisions and suburban cul-de-sacs.

So much for *falls* and other riverine terms, but what about "Gunpowder"? The name occurs not only in Big and Little

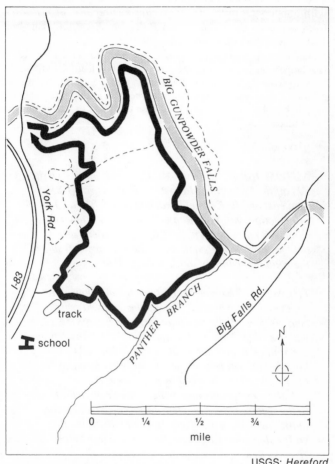

BIG GUNPOWDER FALLS

York Rd.

I-83

track

H school

PANTHER BRANCH

Big Falls Rd.

N

0   ¼   ½   ¾   1
mile

USGS: *Hereford*

Gunpowder Falls but also in Gunpowder Neck, Gunpowder Town (later Joppa), and Gunpowder Island (now Carroll Island). Although most accounts assume that the name originated with gunpowder mills, *The Traveller's Directory, or A Pocket Companion to the Philadelphia-Baltimore Road,* published in 1802, gives the following explanation:

> Great Gunpowder River — Between this and Bush River is Gunpowder Neck, so named from a tradition that the Indians, who formerly lived in this tract, when first acquainted with the use of gunpowder, supposed it to be a vegetable seed; they purchased a quantity and sowed it on this neck, expecting it to produce a good crop.

BUS: None.

AUTOMOBILE: From the Mt. Carmel Road exit (Exit 27) off the Baltimore-Harrisburg Expressway (I-83), turn east on Mt. Carmel Road and then left at a "T" intersection with York Road (Route 45). Follow York Road 1.8 miles north to the Big Gunpowder Falls bridge. Park in the small lot on the left (or west) side of the road immediately south of the bridge.

THE WALK: The walk starts from the meadow at the south end of the bridge. Pick up the trail where it crosses a small stream about forty yards from the water's edge. Nearby is a stone fireplace. Fork left on the South Gunpowder Trail, which is marked by blue blazes. You will return later by the other fork (i.e., by the Panther Trail marked by pink blazes).

Follow the South Gunpowder Trail through the brush to the water's edge. In a few dozen yards, fork right uphill away from the river. Zigzag uphill along the valley slope and ridge and then down again to the river's edge.

With the river on your left, follow the path downstream, generally near the water but sometimes farther up the side of the valley. Fork left at a trail intersection

with Sandy Lane Trail (white dots). Push through an area choked with weeds and undergrowth. Follow the path up a ravine, across a stream, and then up and around to the left above the river. Twenty yards before a large stream (Panther Branch) joins the river from the right, turn very sharply right onto the Panther Branch rail (pink dots). The trail zigzags uphill, over a shoulder, and down to the right. From this point to the end of the walk, follow the pink dots of the Panther Branch Trail.

With Panther Branch on your left, follow the path up the ravine. Climb away to the right to follow a smaller ravine for a short distance before turning left to cross a stream. Continue above Panther Branch. Turn right again up another ravine. Ignore a path by a stone foundation that crosses the stream toward the left. Instead, continue up the ravine with the stream on your left. Eventually veer left across the stream and zigzag uphill to the corner of the Hereford High School track.

Continue straight across a farm field and turn right on a rutted road. Continue straight past a gap in the trees where the road forks. With the field on your right, continue 75 yards and then swerve half-left through another gap in the hedgerow onto a grassy road. Continue with a pine plantation on your left and the hedgerow (and field beyond) on your right.

Follow the dirt road into the woods. Seventy yards after the path turns downhill to the left, leave the dirt road and turn right on the pink dot footpath. Emerge into a clearing and climb half-right to a grassy path in front of another pine plantation. Follow the path right. Continue straight through a grassy crossroads and then turn right in fifteen yards at a trail intersection by the corner of a pine plantation. Follow the pink dots as the trail veers left at the next corner of the pine plantation (instead of proceeding straight downhill on the white dotted Sandy Lane Trail). Turn left again immediately on a narrow footpath through the pines (instead of proceeding straight downhill on the fire lane around the edge of the pines). Follow the footpath down a ravine, across a stream, along the side of the valley, and back to the meadow by the York Road bridge.

10

ROBERT E. LEE PARK

Walking and ski touring — 4 miles (6.4 kilometers). An easy footpath past freshwater marsh, meadow, and woods bordering Lake Roland. A spur trail leads to the serpentine barrens at the eastern end of the Bare Hills. Managed by the Baltimore City Department of Recreation and Parks (396-6106).

BECAUSE OF THE VARIETY of its habitats — bottomland woods, meadows, freshwater marsh, dry piney highlands, and open water — the Robert E. Lee Park (Lake Roland) is particularly popular with birdwatchers, although most of the areas described in this book, even those well within the city, are also good for birding.

About 645 species of birds live and breed in the United States and Canada, but many of these are not found east of the Rocky Mountains. About thirty more species are seen regularly in this country as migrants. In Maryland 348 species have been documented at least three times since 1940. Most, of course, are seen far more often. Another 21 species have been sighted in Maryland once or twice as "accidentals" — or that is, as birds out of their ordinary range.

Identifying these species is easier than might at first be thought. Plumage, shape, size, color, and other physical characteristics provide distinguishing field marks. But just as useful as a bird's appearance are such considerations as range, season, habitat, song, and behavior.

Range is of primary importance for the simple reason that — as has already been intimated — many birds are not found

Marsh at Lake Roland

throughout North America or even the eastern United States; rather, they occur only in certain regions such as the Southeast and Gulf states or across New England, Labrador, northern Canada, and Alaska. For example, cedar waxwings and Bohemian waxwings closely resemble each other, but the latter is not seen in Maryland. The better field guides provide maps of bird ranges based on years of reported sightings and bird counts. Of course, bird ranges are not static. Some pioneering species extend their ranges over time while others lose ground and sometimes disappear altogether.

Related to range is season, inasmuch as migratory birds are found in different parts of their ranges during different times of year. For instance, the spotted breasted thrushes are sometimes difficult to distinguish from each other, but usually only the hermit thrush is present in eastern Maryland during the winter and only the wood thrush is found here during the summer. Swainson's thrush and the gray-cheeked thrush are seen during migration in spring and fall. Again, the maps in most field guides reflect information of this sort. A detailed summation of seasonal occurrence is contained in the *Field List of the Birds of Maryland* by Robbins and Bystrak, available from the Maryland Ornithological Society (see Chapter 17).

Habitat (like range and season) is important because even before you spot a bird you know from the nature of the surroundings what species you are likely to see. Within its range a species is usually found only in certain habitats for which it has a preference and in many cases to which it is physically adapted to some degree, although during migration some species stop over in quite different environments. As its name implies, the long-billed marsh wren is seldom found far from cattails, rushes, sedges, or tall marsh grasses; if a wren-like bird is spotted in such a setting, it is unlikely to be a house wren or Carolina wren or one of the other species that are commonly found in thick underbrush or shrubbery. Similarly, ducks can be difficult to identify unless you tote a telescope, but even if all you can see is a silhouette, you can start with the knowledge that shallow marshes and creeks normally attract few diving ducks (such as

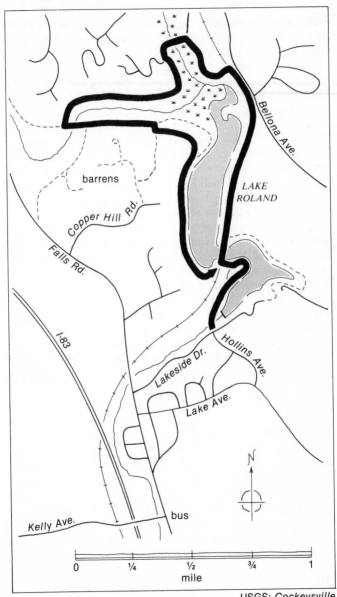

barrens

LAKE
ROLAND

Bellona Ave.

Copper Hill Rd.

Falls Rd.

I-83

Lakeside Dr.

Hollins Ave.

Lake Ave.

N

Kelly Ave.

bus

| 0 | ¼ | ½ | ¾ | 1 |

mile

USGS: *Cockeysville*

redheads, canvasbacks, scaup, goldeneye, and buffleheads) and that large, deep bodies of water are not the usual setting for surface-feeding puddle ducks (mallards, black ducks, pintails, gadwalls, widgeons, shovelers, and teals). Some of the distinctive habitats that provide a home to different bird species are mud flats, beaches, open ocean, sand dunes and brushy hollows, salt marsh, farms, plowed fields, abandoned fields, meadows, pastures, hedgerows, thickets, wood margins, moist coniferous forests, dry piney woods, bottomland and upland deciduous forests, wooded swamps, ponds and creeks, clay banks, freshwater marshes, and open lakes, reservoirs, and estuaries. All good field guides provide information on habitat preference which may be used in locating specific species or in assessing the likelihood of a tentative identification.

Song is another factor that announces the identity (or at least the location) of birds even before they are seen. Some species, such as the red-winged blackbird, have only a few songs, while others, such as the mocking bird, have an infinite variety. In many species the basic songs vary among individuals and also from one area to another, giving rise to regional "dialects." Nonetheless, the vocal repertory of most songbirds is sufficiently constant with respect to timbre and pattern that each species may be recognized simply by its songs.

Bird songs (as distinguished from "calls") can be very complex and in most species are sung only by the male, usually in spring and summer. The male is the first to arrive north on migration. He in effect stakes out a territory for courting, mating, and nesting by singing at various points around the area's perimeter, thus warding off intrusion by other males of his species. Birds tend to heed the songs of their own kind and to ignore the songs of other species, which do not threaten competiton for females or, in many cases, for the same type of nesting materials and food. In consequence, a single area might include the overlapping breeding territories of many species.

As for bird "calls," they are short, sometimes harsh, and made by both males and females at all times of year. Calls are frequently heeded by many species, as in the case of warning calls. Some warnings are thin high-pitched whistles, the source of which is difficult to locate, so that the bird does not disclose its position to a predator simply by sounding the alarm.

Experiments involving young birds that have been deafened indicate that bird songs are inbred only to a very crude extent and that young birds learn their songs by listening to adult birds. So can you. Probably the easiest way is to listen over and over to bird recordings with the simultaneous aid of one of the standard field guides, most of which try to describe bird vocalizations with such terms as *harsh, nasal, flute-like, piercing, plaintive, wavering, twittering, buzzing, sneezy, sputtering,* and on and on.

Shape is one of the first and most important points to notice in a bird once you actually see it. Most birds can at least be placed in the proper family, and many species can be identified by shape or silhouette without reference to other field marks. Some birds, such as the bobwhite or to a lesser extent sparrows, are distinctly chunky, while others, such as catbirds and cuckoos, are more elegantly long and slender. Kingfishers, blue jays, titmice, waxwings, and cardinals are among the small minority of birds with crests.

Bird bills often have distinctive shapes. The bill can be chunky like that of a grosbeak, thin like that of a thrasher, hooked like that of a shrike, or some other characteristic shape depending on the bird's food. In fact, bird beaks probably show more adaptation to food supply than any other single body part.

Other useful elements of body shape are the length and form of wings, tails, and legs. Are the wings long and pointed like those of a falcon (such as a sparrow hawk) or short and rounded like those of an accipiter (such as a sharp-shinned hawk)? Is the tail deeply forked like that of a barn swallow, shallowly notched like that of a tree swallow, square-tipped like that of a cliff swallow, round-tipped like that of a blue jay, pointed like that of a mourning dove, stubby like that of a starling, or long like that of a thrasher?

Size as a factor in identifying birds is of limited usefulness. Although the variation in size among birds of the same species is not great, size is difficult to estimate. The best approach for the birdwatcher is to bear in mind the relative sizes of different species and to use certain well-known birds — chickadee, song sparrow, robin, kingfisher, crow, and so forth — as standards for purposes of discussion or mental comparison. For example, if a bird resembles a song sparrow but looks unusually large, it might be a fox sparrow. Also, despite the marked difference in shape and plumage, a cardinal might conveniently be described as robin-sized, or a grackle as longer-tailed than a robin.

Plumage, whether plain or princely, muted or magnificent, is one of the most obvious keys to identification. Color can occur in remarkable combinations of spots, stripes, streaks, patches, and other patterns that make even supposedly drab birds a pleasure to see. To organize this variation, focus on different basic elements. Starting with the head, is it uniformly colored as in the red-headed woodpecker? Is there a small patch on the crown as in Wilson's warbler or the ruby-crowned kinglet, or a larger cap on the front and top of the head as in the common redpoll and American goldfinch? Is the crown striped like that of an ovenbird? Does a ring surround the eye, as in a Connecticut warbler, or are the eye rings perhaps even joined across the top of the bill to form spectacles, as in a yellow-breasted chat? Is there a stripe over or through the eyes, as in the red-breasted nuthatch, or a conspicuous black mask across the eyes, like that of a yellowthroat or loggerhead shrike? From the head go on to the rest of the body, where distinctive colors and patterns can also mark a bird's bill, throat, breast, belly, back, sides, wings, rump, tail, and legs.

Finally, what a bird *does* is an important clue to its identity. Certain habits, postures, ways of searching for food, and other behavior are characteristic of different species. Some birds, such as juncos and towhees, are strictly ground feeders; others, including swallows and flycatchers, nab insects on the wing; and still others, such as nuthatches, creepers, and woodpeckers, glean insects from the crevices in bark. Vireos and most warblers pick insects from the foliage of trees and brush. All of these birds may be further distinguished by other habits of eating. For example, towhees scratch for insects and seeds by kicking backward with both feet together, whereas juncos rarely do, although both groups move on the ground by hopping. Still other ground feeders (such as meadowlarks) walk rather than hop. Swallows catch insects while swooping and skimming in continuous flight, whereas flycatchers dart out from a limb, grab an insect (sometimes with an audible smack), and then return to their perch. Brown creepers have the curious habit of systematically searching for food by climbing trees in spirals, then flying back to the ground to climb again. Woodpeckers tend to hop upward, bracing themselves with their stiff tails. Nuthatches walk up and down trees and branches head first, seemingly without regard for gravity or blood pressure. And, vireos are sluggish compared to the hyperactive, flitting warblers.

Different species not only have different characteristic habits of feeding but also different styles of flight. Soaring is typical of some big birds. Gulls float nearly motionless in the wind. Buteos and turkey vultures glide on updrafts in wide circles, although turkey vultures may be further distinguished by the shallow "V" in which they hold their wings. Some other large birds, such as accipiters, rarely soar but instead interrupt their wingbeats with glides. Sparrow hawks, kingfishers, and terns can hover in one spot. Hummingbirds, like oversized dragonflies, can also hover and can even fly backwards. Slightly more erratic than the swooping, effortless flight of swallows is that of swifts, flitting with wing beats that appear to alternate (but do not). Still other birds, such as the goldfinch and flicker, dip up and down in wavelike flight. And, some species, including blue jays and grackles, have no more imagination than to fly dead straight. Among ducks, the surface feeding species launch themselves directly upward into flight, seeming to jump from the water, whereas the heavy diving ducks typically patter along the surface before becoming airborne.

Other bird species are distinguished by yet other idiosyncracies. The spotted sandpiper and northern waterthrush walk with a teetering, bobbing motion. Coots pump their heads back and forth as they swim. A phoebe regularly jerks its tail downward while perching, whereas wrens often cock their tails vertically. Herons fly with their necks folded back, while other large waders keep their necks extended. Still other birds have characteristic postures while sitting or flying or other unique habits that provide a reliable basis for identification.

BUS: From downtown take the MTA Fallstaff & Sanzo roads bus or the Belvedere & Belview bus (both # 10) via Howard Street and Falls Road to Mt. Washington Village at the intersection of Falls Road and Kelly Avenue. You will know that your stop is coming after you pass Northern Parkway.

From Mt. Washington Village walk north half a mile on Falls Road to the park entrance at Lakeside Drive, which intersects from the right immediately before the viaduct over Jones Falls. Follow Lakeside Drive into the park to the intersection with Hollins Avenue. Do not be alarmed if this road is closed to vehicles; it is open to pedestrians.

AUTOMOBILE: From the Jones Falls Expressway (I-83) take Northern Parkway eastward and then Falls Road 0.8 mile northward to Lake Avenue. The park entrance is on Hollins Avenue, which intersects with Lake Avenue 0.5 mile east of Falls Road. Follow Hollins to Lakeside Drive.

From the intersection of Lakeside Drive and Hollins Avenue inside the park, parking areas may be reached by following Lakeside Drive to the right of the dam.

THE WALK: Start your walk at the intersection of Lakeside Drive and Hollins Avenue inside the park. Cross the bridge just below the dam. Follow the asphalt path, at one point forking right along the water's edge. Just beyond a stone pavilion located at the top of the knoll, follow a dirt path downhill to the right. Continue on the dirt path to the southern end of the railroad bridge that cuts across Lake

Dame's Rocket, Hesperis matronalis

*Roland, formerly Baltimore's water supply. Watch for
trains, since the railroad is still in use.*

*Follow the railroad across the reservoir and northward
for approximately three-quarters of a mile. Bellona
Avenue (named for the Bellona Gunpowder Mill that
formerly stood in this area) runs parallel to the tracks for
part of the distance. Although this portion of the walk is
unattractive, it is soon over and the rest is very pleasant.*

*When Bellona Avenue veers uphill to the right away
from the railroad, leave the tracks and turn left on one of
several footpaths leading to a field. Follow the left edge of
the field, which at one point overlooks a freshwater marsh
through which meanders Roland Run.*

*Continue through the meadow as it narrows until you
reach a road opposite a tennis court. Follow the road left
across a small bridge and around the corner to the left.
Forty yards from the corner, fork left onto a footpath, with
the stream and marsh on the left and a few houses on the
right. Follow the narrow streamside footpath as it curves
right and winds through the streamside jungle, eventually
reaching an abandoned railroad bridge across Jones
Falls.*

*Turn left across the bridge. Continue straight past a
path leading uphill to the right about 120 yards beyond the
bridge. Follow the broad path as it winds easily through
the woods. Immediately after the trail swerves abruptly to
the right, turn left at a trail intersection. The other trail
leads uphill to a dry, rocky, elevated portion of the park
entirely different in character from the dense, wet woodland around the lake. You may want to follow this side path
for a short distance and back just to examine the piney
serpentine highlands, similar to the Soldiers Delight area
discussed in Chapter 6.*

*Continuing on the lower path, the main body of Lake
Roland eventually comes into view on the left. Follow the
path back to the railroad bridge across the lake. Cross the*

tracks and follow the dirt path uphill to the knoll and stone pavilion where you started.

As the map shows, there is also a path of sorts around the southern portion of Lake Roland, but it is not recommended. The path is at times too steep, confused, and ill-maintained to be enjoyable.

11

LOCH RAVEN
Southern Shore

Walking and ski touring — 6 miles (9.7 kilometers). An easy dirt road that winds around the hillsides and ravines at the southern end of Loch Raven. For the most part the trail is through high-canopied deciduous forest. Several spur trails lead to the shore. Managed by the Baltimore City Bureau of Water and Wastewater (795-6151).

LOCH RAVEN IS ONE OF Baltimore City's three major reservoirs. The others are Prettyboy Reservoir, located upstream from Loch Raven on the Big Gunpowder Falls, and Liberty Reservoir, on the North Branch of the Patapsco River. Both Loch Raven and Liberty are terminal reservoirs — the last impoundments on their rivers before the water is removed and treated for drinking. Prettyboy Reservoir simply provides additional storage within the Gunpowder watershed. When the level of Loch Raven drops more than three feet below the crest of the dam, water is released from Prettyboy in order to maintain high water in Loch Raven. As a result, the level of Prettyboy Reservoir fluctuates widely, as does the water in the Big Gunpowder Falls above and below Loch Raven, depending on whether the reservoirs are being filled or spilled. As an additional supply,

Canada geese, Loch Raven

Baltimore has the right to pump water from the Philadelphia Electric Company's Conowingo Dam on the Susquehanna River, but it has done so only in droughts or other emergencies.

To protect its water supply, Baltimore City owns about nine square miles of forested land surrounding each of its three reservoirs. In managing these buffer areas, the city has adopted a multiple-use policy that includes the harvesting of timber for municipal projects and that also allows a wide variety of recreational uses.

Timber cutting began on Baltimore's watershed properties in 1948, when the city decided to use the trees standing in the area that would soon be flooded by the new Liberty Dam. The city hired a woods crew and purchased logging equipment and even a saw mill. Selective cutting of hardwood trees has continued ever since to supply the Department of Public Works and other city departments with both crude and finished lumber, including shoring for trenches, fence posts, guardrails, pier timbers, and survey stakes. The city also harvests and sells pulpwood thinned from its watershed pine plantations. As of 1980, the value of the lumber and pulpwood cut from the city's watersheds was averaging about $200,000 per year.

The city's timber program is designed to avoid erosion and to minimize the unsightliness commonly associated with logging. Clear-cutting, even in small areas, is rarely done. During wet weather logging is stopped. Streams, roadsides, and shorelines are avoided. In areas that are heavily used by the public, logging is limited to salvaging dead or damaged trees. Yet despite these and other precautions, the city often receives complaints from dismayed preservationists urging that the forests should not be touched.

Although Baltimore's watershed properties are not public parks, the city also tries, as a part of its multiple-use policy, to accommodate recreational activities that are compatible with the higher priorities of water protection and forest management. Permitted activites include fishing, hiking, horseback riding, and bow-and-arrow hunting at Prettyboy and Liberty Reservoirs, and skeet shooting and golf at Loch Raven. One thousand boat

USGS: Towson

Raven Rd.

Providence Rd.

Loch

Dulaney Valley Rd.

Seminary Ave.

bus

N

mile

0   ¼   ½   ¾   1

permits are distributed annually by lottery, but no gasoline motors or sailboats are allowed. Rowboats can be rented at the Loch Raven Fishing Center off Dulaney Valley Road.

This range of recreation is liberal compared to activities permitted on other municipal reservoirs in the East. According to a survey conducted in 1968 by the United States Forest Service's Northeastern Forest Experiment Station, boating was allowed at only 11 percent of municipal reservoirs in the Northeast and Mid-Atlantic region, fishing at 39 percent, picnicking at 19 percent, hiking at 35 percent, horseback riding at 14 percent, and hunting in general at 40 percent. Camping and swimming, both prohibited at Baltimore's reservoirs, were permitted respectively at 9 percent and 4 percent of reservoirs. Baltimore's watershed managers, however, point out that opportunities for camping and swimming are already available at state and county parks near Baltimore.

Whether recreation on reservoirs or in their surrounding watersheds actually impairs water quality is unknown. What little research has been done has produced inconclusive results. But other management problems caused by large numbers of visitors are only too clear. Baltimore, for example, has closed indefinitely its picnic area at Loch Raven and has curtailed use of the Liberty Dam overlook because crowds and drinking were getting out of hand. Also, litter is pervasive, thrown overboard from boats, scattered at fishing spots along the shore, and heaped at focal spots such as the trailhead below Prettyboy Dam. Even horseback riding has become a nuisance in some places as dirt roads have been kneaded into quagmires and gullies. In the Forest Service survey noted earlier, over a third of the managers of watersheds where recreation was permitted indicated that recreation caused serious problems.

Recreational use of reservoirs and watersheds also increases administrative burdens. Areas popular with visitors have to be patrolled more often to enforce watershed regulations. Only recently has a citation system been developed for offenders. Although much of the responsibility for overseeing the wide range of programs at Baltimore's reservoirs has fallen on the city's Watershed Section, some of the administrative duties have been given to other agencies with a more immediate interest in public recreation. The Baltimore City Department of Recreation and Parks operates the skeet range and golf course at Loch Raven, and the Baltimore County Department of Recreation and Parks runs the Loch Raven boat rental and fishing concession. Similarly, state Fish and Wildlife Administration officers assist in enforcing the city's ban on firearms. Even so, the Watershed Section has reserved the right to curtail any use or practice that adversely affects water quality, as proved necessary when it was discovered that the city's Department of Recreation and Parks was using a mercury-based fungicide at the Pine Ridge Golf Course along the shore of Loch Raven.

BUS: From downtown, take the MTA Stella Maris bus (#8) via Greenmount Avenue and York Road through Towson. Tell the driver that you want to get off at the intersection of Dulaney Valley Road and Seminary Avenue. You will know that your stop is coming as the bus heads downhill after crossing the Beltway (I-695) and passes St. Francis Road on the right. Flag the bus for the return trip. Several other MTA buses (9, 18, 26) either cross or follow Seminary Avenue not far to the west of the walk's starting point.

AUTOMOBILE: The trail entrance is near some dirt parking spaces on the north side of Seminary Avenue 150 yards east of the intersection with Dulaney Valley Road (Route 146). This intersection is located 0.8 mile north of the Dulaney Valley Road exit (Exit 27) off the Beltway (I-695). The eastern end of the trail is also accessible from the intersection of Providence Road and Loch Raven Road.

THE WALK: Start your walk on the dirt road entering the woods under the overhead wires on the north side of Seminary Avenue, 150 yards east of the intersection with Dulaney Valley Road. Cross a small stream and follow the

*path uphill. Continue on the main trail past two grassy
paths leading left. At a fork in the trail, bear right. (The
left-hand fork splits in a short distance and each branch —
the right branch is better — leads to the water's edge.)
Continue on the main path as the forest becomes more
mature — i.e., the trees get taller and the understory less
choked with vines and scrubby growth. Continue straight
where another path leads right uphill shortly before a
small stream. Bear right at a fork in the trail past a large
tree with three trunks; you will return by the other fork
later. Follow the path uphill, then down. Part way down
the hill, double back uphill on a trail intersecting from the
left. Follow the woods road around and down to the trail
junction passed earlier. Return by the way you came to the
intersection with Seminary Avenue and Dulaney Valley
Road.*

May Apple, Podophyllum peltatum

12

LOCH RAVEN
Southeast Narrows and Highlands

Walking — 5 miles (8 kilometers). Broad views over the reservoir from Loch Raven Road and bridge No. 1, closed to motor vehicles on Saturdays and Sundays between 10 a.m. and 5 p.m. Continue on an easy circuit through the woods high above the water. A spur trail leads through a deep ravine to a promontory north of the dam. Not reachable by public transportation. Managed by the Baltimore City Bureau of Water and Wastewater (795-6151).

ALTHOUGH BALTIMORE CITY OWNS about nine square miles of watershed land surrounding each of its three reservoirs, its property amounts to less than 6 percent of the 303 square miles in the Big Gunpowder Falls drainage area above Loch Raven dam and also less than 6 percent of the 164 square miles in the Patapsco watershed above Liberty Dam. No part of these two drainage areas is within the city. The resulting lack of control over the watershed greatly complicates protection of Baltimore's water supply.

Sedimentation, for example, is a major problem traceable largely to erosion on land that is not controlled by the city. The lower reaches of both the Patapsco and Gunpowder rivers were quickly filled with silt after the European settlement, when most of the interior was cleared for tobacco plantations. Sheet erosion and the downstream deposition of topsoil were so great that by the early 19th century the ports of Elkridge Landing on the Patapsco and Joppatown on the Gunpowder could no longer be reached by boats drawing more than two or three feet.

Annually cultivated cropland still contributes about half of the nearly one million tons of sediment — the equivalent of 20,000 freight cars full — that wash into the waters of the Baltimore area yearly, filling the various reservoirs that have been built throughout the region. Lake Roland, a city reservoir from 1862 to 1915, was dredged repeatedly during that period. After its discontinuance as a reservoir, the lake lost 40 percent of its volume to sedimentation by 1946 and another 20 percent by 1974. Erosion from farmland not only clogs streams and reduces the storage capacity of reservoirs but also increases turbidity and pollution from fertilizers, animal wastes, and pesticides with which the mud is permeated.

A series of surveys conducted at Loch Raven and Prettyboy reservoirs reveals wide fluctuations in the rate of sedimentation, perhaps reflecting major changes in land use and development practices throughout the watershed. A survey made in 1943 indicated that the average rate of sediment production per acre for the entire drainage area above Loch Raven was forty-two cubic feet per year. The figures for the drainage area above Prettyboy Reservoir were even higher. Much of this, of course, was from streambank cutting rather than sheet erosion from cultivated fields. Nonetheless, the engineer who conducted the survey recommended that soil conservation techniques such as contour plowing, strip cropping, terracing, and gully control be put into effect promptly on the watershed's farmlands.

In 1961 another survey indicated that the average annual rate of sediment accumulation above Loch Raven for the period since 1943 had fallen by 70 percent. The Soil Conservation

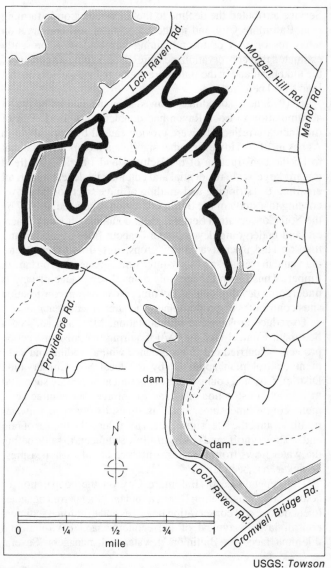

USGS: *Towson*

Service attributed the decline to the great reduction in farming near Baltimore City and to the adoption of soil conservation measures on part of the remaining farmland. It is presently estimated that conservation measures used on only 32 percent of the total farmland in the Baltimore region reduce soil loss on that land by 80 percent.

In 1973 new soundings showed that the rate of sediment accumulation in Loch Raven had doubled since 1961. Part of this increase reflected severe erosion caused by tropical storm Agnes in 1972. However, other significant factors were thought to be the construction of the Beltway and I-83 and the trend toward large-scale residential and commercial development, all entailing the stripping and grading of huge tracts of land. According to a study of the Baltimore region conducted in 1977 by the Soil Conservation Service, the amount of soil loss per acre on land undergoing development is about fifteen times greater than on land in cultivated row crops, forty-four times greater than land in pasture, and sixty-three times greater than on land in timber. Thus, even though only a small percentage of land is undergoing development at any time, erosion from construction sites contributes disproportionately to stream sedimentation.

To reduce erosion and sedimentation, Maryland adopted a Sediment Control Law in 1970 requiring that all construction projects be carried out in accordance with a grading and sediment control plan approved by the local Soil Conservation District. City and county building permit agencies are supposed to inspect construction sites and to enforce the required sediment control measures, such as dikes to divert stormwater runoff around the site, straw mulch to cushion the impact of rain and to slow runoff, and basins to allow sediments to settle before the water flows from the sites. Enforcement of such measures, however, has been lax.

The dependence of Baltimore City on the cooperation of county Soil Conservation Districts and building permit agencies to encourage soil conservation practices and to enforce sediment control laws is typical of the economic and environmental dilemma faced by Baltimore's watershed managers. Several jurisdictions are involved, and often a cheap solution for one area's wastewater problem imposes injury and expense on another. For example, in 1972 tests conducted by the federal Environmental Protection Agency indicated that algae growth in Loch Raven was rampant, stimulated in part by phosphates in the effluent from the Manchester and Hampstead sewage treatment plants in Carroll County. Equipment to remove some of the phosphorus was not installed until five years later, after Baltimore City, Baltimore County, Carroll County, and the state contributed the necessary funds.

A comprehensive and coordinated program to combat water pollution is the object of the Baltimore Region Water Quality Management Plan prepared by the Regional Planning Council under Section 208 of the federal Clean Water Act of 1972. County and municipal governments in the region have been designated as water quality management agencies in order to receive federal grants to improve wastewater treatment facilities. Also, "lead agencies" (such as the Baltimore County Health Department) have been designated to coordinate local efforts to monitor and improve water quality. At the state level the Office of Environmental Programs reviews and enforces industrial and municipal discharge permits based on state and federal standards for clean water. To protect drinking water in particular, a Reservoir Watershed Management Program has been established by agreement among Baltimore City and Baltimore and Carroll Counties. Perhaps inevitably, the program's first step has been to undertake a further study of the problem.

Another form of county prerogative that has a major impact on Baltimore City's water supply is zoning. As more of Baltimore County has joined the city's water system, the county has exercised its zoning power to steer intensive development away from tributary streams and other sensitive watershed areas. Representatives from the city's Bureau of Water and Wastewater served on an advisory committee in 1976 when Baltimore County established a new Watershed Protection Zone covering areas near reservoirs and large tributaries. As of 1981 the minimum lot size in the Watershed Protection Zone was three acres, but parcels exceeding ten acres could only be subdivided at an average density of at least five acres per lot.

Yet another difficulty of watershed protection is reflected in the distinction between point source and non-point source pollution. A point source is literally a specific major source that can be pointed at, such as a factory that does not meet clean water standards. In contrast, contaminants which come from widespread, myriad sources — such as sediments from erosion — are non-point pollution. On a cumulative basis, non-point pollution may equal or exceed that from point sources, while being much more intractable. Not surprisingly, most clean-up efforts so far have been directed at eliminating pollution from readily identifiable point sources. For example, Manchester and Hampstead are being pressed to reduce still further the level of phosphates and other nutrients in their sewage effluent, even though most such contaminants in the Big Gunpowder Falls are thought to come from inadequate private septic systems and from fertilizers and animal wastes from farmland throughout the region.

Stormwater runoff from suburban developments, towns and cities is another form of non-point pollution. Not only is surface runoff from such areas contaminated with oil residues, toxic metals, and other wastes, but also the sheer volume of runoff is increased by the development of land. Experiments conducted at Liberty Reservoir indicate that when land is cleared of trees and planted in grass, annual runoff increases up to 30 percent because less water is returned to the atmosphere through transpiration and evaporation from leaf and bark surfaces. Similarly, large impervious surfaces such as roofs, roads, and parking lots intercept water that to some extent would have soaked into the ground. Instead, storm sewers quickly flush the water into streams, loading the rivers with filth, swelling peak volumes, and increasing erosive energy. To prevent this surge of stormwater runoff, some environmentalists are urging that subdivision requirements for extensive storm sewers, gutters, and curbs be relaxed, and that instead greater use be made of permeable riprap drainage swales and infiltration basins to slow stormwater

runoff, filter out dirt and debris, and increase percolation into the ground.

BUS: None.

AUTOMOBILE: The walk starts at the intersection of Providence and Loch Raven roads, located 2.5 miles northwest on Providence Road from Exit 28 off the Beltway (I-695). Park on Providence Road.

THE WALK: From the intersection of Providence and Loch Raven roads, follow Loch Raven Road north so that the reservoir soon comes into view on the right. About 400 yards after the bridge (and opposite where pines begin to appear on the left) turn right on a trail leading into the woods. Turn right again immediately and follow the dirt road up the side of a gully. Turn right at a trail intersection and follow the path up and over a hill and then around to the left, with the land sloping off to the right toward the water. Eventually turn right at a four-way trail inter-section.

Follow the path up a gradual hill along a low ridge. Pass a trail leading downhill to the right (unless you want to explore the isolated promontory north of the dam). Turn left at the next rail junction and follow the path gradually downhill and then around to the right. Turn left at a trail junction and continue to Loch Raven Road.

13

GUNPOWDER FALLS STATE PARK
Belair Road to Harford Road

Walking and ski touring — up to 9 miles (14.5 kilometers) round trip. An easy footpath along the river bank through a deep and isolated valley. Although close to the city and the surrounding suburbia, this canyon is a remarkable wilderness enclave. Continue as far as you want and return by the way you came. Managed by the Maryland Park Service (592-2897).

THIS WALK IS THE FIRST OF three starting at the Belair Road bridge and focusing on the stretch of Big Gunpowder Falls below Loch Raven dam. Upstream on the south bank the riverside path extends to the Harford Road bridge through one of the deepest parts of the Big Gunpowder gorge. On the north bank above Belair Road the circle path explores the valley slopes and upland. And, the downstream circuit follows the river toward the edge of the fall line zone where the Gunpowder leaves its Piedmont valley and enters the Coastal Plain. Throughout the length of all three excursions, the valley slopes are covered with deep woods. The river itself at high water is swift, powerful, and sometimes turbulent. At low water (or no water) its bed is a broad, bare swath of cobbles and boulders.

If by now you have taken some of the walks outlined in this book, you have probably noticed a certain sameness in our local landscape. With the exception of Anne Arundel County, the countryside in the Baltimore region is characterized by rolling uplands dissected by an intricate system of ravines, valleys, and gorges. This landscape provides as good an example as any of the erosional cycle by which running water carves into an elevated region and over the ages reduces it to a low plain.

Stream erosion is the dominant force at work shaping the world's landforms. Whenever any part of the earth's crust is raised above sea level, either by uplift of the land or withdrawal of the ocean as water is amassed in continental glaciers, the newly elevated surface is at once attacked by the erosive power of water. Any downward pitched trough, crevice, or fissure, even though at first shallow or insignificant, is self-aggrandizing, collecting to itself rainwater that falls on other areas. At first such minor watercourses are dry between rains, but gradually they are deepened by erosion. Once they penetrate the water table, they are fed by a steady seepage of ground water from the sides of the ravines.

As a stream extends itself by developing tributaries, its erosive power rapidly increases. The larger drainage area concentrates more water in the channel downstream, where stream energy is swelled both by the greater mass of moving water and also by its greater depth, which results in proportionately less friction with the streambed. In consequence, the speed of the river increases and so does its ability to pick up fine clay, silt, and sand in suspension and to push and roll pebbles and cobbles downstream.

Although at first erosion is fastest where volume is greatest in the lower reaches of a river, the ocean constitutes a base level below which the stream cannot cut to any significant degree. As downward cutting approaches the base level, the site of the most rapid erosion slowly moves upstream.

Meanwhile, the lower river still possesses great energy which is applied to eroding the bank wherever the stream is deflected by each slight turn. This tendency to carve wider and wider

curves is present along the entire stream, but it is accentuated in the lower reaches where downward cutting is no longer possible but where sideward cutting can continue as long as there is flow. Gradually, a meandering course develops as the river snakes back and forth, gnawing first at one side of the valley and then the other. When sinuosity becomes so extreme that the river doubles back on itself, the current will intercept the channel farther downstream, cutting off the looping meander. Thus, over the course of time the river migrates in an ever-changing, winding course over the bottomland, creating a valley much wider than it is deep and leaving behind abandoned channels here and there.

Yet another distinctive geologic feature develops at the mouth of the river where it empties into an ocean, bay, or lake. As the current dissipates in the standing water, the capacity of the stream to carry material in suspension is reduced and then eliminated, so that the river's load of gravel, sand, and silt is dropped and forms a delta. Because of the gradual slowing of the current, the deposition tends to be self-sorting, with the larger particles dropped first (all very convenient for the sand and gravel companies that mine these areas). After the delta has extended itself a considerable distance in one direction, a flood may cut a new and shorter channel to open water, causing the former course to be abandoned, at least for a period. Deltas typically have a variety of channels among which the stream shifts as deposition is concentrated first in one and then in another.

By focusing on the variables of stream gradient, valley depth, valley width, and number of meanders, you can classify any stretch of river in terms of its stage of development. In the earliest stage the gradient of the streambed is relatively steep. Rapids are common. Because the dominant direction of cutting is downward, valleys and ravines are steep-sided and V-shaped. There are no meanders and no flats in the valley bottoms. Valley depth relative to width is maximized. Such a stream is said to be in its *youth*.

USGS: *White Marsh*

parking
bus
Belair Rd.
Forge Rd.
bus Perry Hall
BIG GUNPOWDER FALLS
Harford Rd.
Long Factory Rd.

N
mile
0   1/4   1/2   3/4   1

As the stream approaches base level, its gradient diminishes and downward cutting slows. The bends in the course of the stream become accentuated, and the width of the valley increases relative to its depth. Beginning at the point where sideward cutting becomes significant and a flat valley floor starts to develop, the stream is said to be in its *maturity*.

Finally, when downward cutting has ceased and the stream is at base level, sideward cutting produces a nearly flat and featureless valley, much wider than it is deep, across which the river meanders from side to side. Such an erosional surface is called a *peneplain*. The gradient is low and the broad bottomland is marked only by the scars, swamps, and lakes left by former channels and perhaps also a few rock hummocks and hills more resistant to erosion than their surroundings. This stage of river development is *old age*.

Of course, the terms *old age* and *maturity* can best be applied only to sections of a river. Every stream becomes more youthful upstream, so that the uppermost valleys of a river and its tributaries will always be in youth. Also, these terms do not describe the actual age of a stream but only its stage of development. Some streams develop faster than others depending on the climate of the area, the resistance of the underlying rock to erosion, and other geologic events.

The same terms — youth, maturity, and old age — can also be used to characterize for an entire landscape or region the extent to which it has been acted upon by stream erosion. As a region is dissected by the headward erosion of a stream system, more and more of the landscape is given over to a branching network of steep-sided valleys, ravines, and gullies, which gradually widen and develop flat valley bottoms. Focusing on the ratio among original upland, valley slope, and valley bottom, an area is said to be in youth until about half of the original upland is consumed by valley slopes and the streams are just beginning to develop flats at the valley bottoms. As the percentage of upland diminishes further and the portion in valley flats increases, the area is in maturity. At some point the upland lying between different tributaries or different stream systems is

cut away until the divide changes from a wide flat summit to a sharp-crested ridge that in turn is worn down to a low rounded rise. Old age is said to start when more than half of the region is in valley bottom; it continues as the whole region is gradually reduced to a peneplain. Thus, in general, youth is the time of dominant upland, maturity the time of dominant valley slope, and old age the time of dominant valley bottom.

Such is the way an idealized stream develops. Turning to the Maryland landscape at hand, as you approach the Gunpowder Falls and walk along the river or through any of the stream valleys discussed in this book, study the landscape to determine the degree to which it conforms to the pattern outlined here.

BUS: From downtown take the MTA Kingsville or Perry Hall bus (both #15A) via Calvert Street, North Avenue, and Belair Road northeast out of the city. On weekdays you can ride all the way to the Gunpowder River. Tell the driver well in advance that you want to get off at the bridge. You will know that your stop is coming as the road descends into the wooded valley after passing Perry Hall Road on the right. When you get off the bus, tell the driver to be expecting your return later in the day. For the return trip flag the bus from the wide gravel shoulder south of the bridge. On Saturday bus 15A goes only to Perry Hall, and you must walk 1.5 miles north on Belair Road to the river.

AUTOMOBILE: From the Beltway (I-695) Belair Road (Route 1) crosses Gunpowder Falls 5.4 miles northeast of Beltway Exit 32 North. A gravel parking area is located at the south end of the bridge on the downstream side. You will know that the bridge and pullout are coming when the road descends into the wooded river valley.

THE WALK: Facing upstream and starting thirty yards away from the south end of the Belair Road bridge, follow a gravel drive briefly downhill. Continue straight on a faint footpath through tall grass. Cross a stream and follow a narrow footpath through the woods and eventually to the river, where the path widens. You may pass several log or rock hurdles erected by local residents to discourage trailbikers.

With the water on your right, follow the riverside footpath for as long as you care to walk, keeping in mind that you will be returning by the same route. The path stretches 4.5 miles to Harford Road. After passing to the right of a brick structure and electric substation, the trail becomes a dirt and gravel road. Near Harford Road the trail fords a stream which in high water may more easily be crossed on the rocks a few dozen yards upstream.

The Gunpowder Falls State Park headquarters is on the north bank of the river a short distance below the Harford Road bridge. A few hundred yards farther downstream are the remains of the Gunpowder Copper Works, which operated between 1804 and 1883. The roof of the original dome of the national Capitol was rolled and fabricated here from blocks of copper imported from Wales.

14

GUNPOWDER FALLS STATE PARK
Stockdale Road and Valley Rim

*Walking — 3.5 miles (5.6 kilometers). From Belair Road up-
stream along the side of the valley on old Stockdale Road, a
gravel and dirt path closed to motor vehicles. Return along the
valley rim on dirt roads and footpaths through former farmland
now planted in pines. A spur trail leads a short distance to the
cascades on Long Green Creek. Managed by the Maryland
Park Service (592-2897).*

IN TERMS OF THE STAGES of stream development discussed
in the preceding chapter, the stretch of the Big Gunpowder Falls
traversed by this walk is still young, perhaps bordering on
maturity. The river flows in a steep-sided valley. Narrow strips
of bottomland flats occur only at intervals along the banks.
Although the gorge itself twists and turns, the channel does not
meander but rather is confined by the valley walls.

However, three miles below the Belair Road bridge the river
leaves its rocky Piedmont valley and flows out over the Coastal
Plain, which is composed of gravel, sand, and clay deposited as
marine sediments during periods when the region was sub-
merged beneath the ocean. As would be expected, the relative

ease of erosion in the soft sediments has enabled the rivers that cross the coastal zone to advance rapidly into maturity and even old age. For example, when the Big Gunpowder Falls reaches the Coastal Plain, the valley walls dwindle and disappear. The river flows slowly within mud and gravel banks over a broad lowland marked by former channels that are now located far from the present course of the river. The Gunpowder even has had time to develop a large delta in the vicinity of Days Cove. The sand and gravel beds here are so valuable that planners for the Gunpowder Falls State Park have concluded that the state cannot afford to buy the area until the owners have completed mining the deposits.

Marking the transition beween Piedmont and Coastal Plain is the so-called fall line, which is not really a sharp line but is rather a zone of considerable width. Within the fall line zone the uplands are covered by a tapering layer of Coastal Plain sediments, but the stream channels penetrate into the underlying Piedmont rocks. Also, waterfalls and rapids are not confined to the fall zone but frequently extend dozens of miles upstream, as is the case on the Gunpowder Falls and Patapsco River. In Maryland the tracks of the Baltimore & Ohio Railroad follow the edge of the fall zone because the route combines level terrain with narrow river crossings.

Although in most respects the Big Gunpowder Falls conforms to the pattern of stream development discussed in the preceding chapter, several anomalies exist. One curiosity is that some of the Gunpowder's tributary valleys, such as the Dulaney and Cockeysville valleys, have smooth, broad (in other words, *old*) profiles compared to the relatively youthful main gorge farther downstream, even though the tributaries necessarily are of more recent origin than the section of the river below them. The tributaries, it turns out, flow through areas underlaid by Cockeysville marble, which (because it is limestone) dissolves more easily than the gneiss, serpentine, granite, gabbro, and other hard crystalline rocks that predominate throughout the region. Thus the terrain along a river can reflect different stages of erosional development in no particular sequence, depending on the underlying rock.

Mt. Vista Rd.

Mohr Rd.

Belair Rd.

bus

parking

Stockdale Rd.

SWEATHOUSE BRANCH

LONG GREEN CREEK

Harford Rd.

BIG GUNPOWDER FALLS

N

0   1/4   1/2   3/4   1
mile

The variety of rock types, their different degrees of resistance to erosion, and the complications in their structural relations may also have contributed to some of the abrupt twists and turns that occur in the valley of the Big Gunpowder Falls. For the most part, however, the Gunpowder and its many tributaries show the spreading rootlike pattern of a dendritic stream system, as is typical in areas where there is no systematic rock structure that guides the pattern of erosion.

Another anomaly is evident in Maryland's Piedmont upland, which consists of rolling hills characteristic of a mature stream system. Yet this landscape is further dissected by a youthful system of gorges and ravines. The cause appears to be that the entire Piedmont, after being shaped by erosion into a region of moderate, rounded ridges and broad valleys, was uplifted. The rise of the land increased stream gradients and renewed the ability of rivers to erode downward. As a result, youthful gorges were cut into the old surface, producing the present landscape in which the gentle slopes and broad bottomlands of the former valleys remain as elevated shoulders above the entrenched gorges. In the terminology of geologists, such a process of regional uplift and renewed erosion is called *rejuvenation*.

There is evidence in Maryland and along the East Coast that the uplift of the Piedmont has not progressed at a steady rate relative to sea level, which itself has fluctuated as water has been consumed and then released by the formation and melting of successive continental glaciers. After each uplift the land along the coast was exposed to the horizontal cutting action of waves and meandering rivers. In consequence, on a regional scale the topography of both the Piedmont and the Coastal Plain roughly forms a flight of terracelike surfaces that parallel the coast and even extend upstream in the major river valleys.

BUS: From downtown take the MTA Kingsville or Perry Hall bus (both #15A) via Calvert Street, North Avenue, and Belair Road northeast out of the city. On weekdays you can ride all the way to the Gunpowder River. Tell the driver well in advance that you want to get off at the bridge.

You will know that your stop is coming as the road descends into the wooded river valley after passing Perry Hall Road on the right. When you get off the bus, tell the driver to be expecting your return later in the day. For the return trip flag the bus from the wide gravel shoulder south of the bridge. On Saturday bus 15A goes only as far as Perry Hall, and you must walk 1.5 miles north on Belair Road to the river.

AUTOMOBILE: From the Beltway (I-695), Belair Road (Route 1) crosses Gunpowder Falls 5.4 miles northeast of Beltway Exit 32 North. A gravel parking area is located at the south end of the bridge on the downstream side. You will know that the bridge and pullout are coming when the road descends into the wooded river valley.

THE WALK: Start your walk on the wide path entering the woods at the north end of the Belair Road bridge. With the river on your left, follow the riverside path upstream for nearly a mile. Fork right uphill away from the river. (The path that continues along the river eventually crosses Sweathouse Branch and then continues as a narrow trail for a few hundred yards to Long Green Creek.)

Follow the path as it climbs and curves to the right. Pass through a pine plantation marking an area which at the time the park was acquired was field or meadow. At a "T" intersection turn right and then left in a few hundred yards to continue through the pine plantation. Pass a path intersecting from the left and continue downhill through deciduous woods.

As you approach two houses located on a gravel road, turn right back into the woods on a path starting next to a log foundation, or cribbing. Fork right after a third of a mile and continue through the woods to a pine plantation on the left. At a "T" intersection turn right downhill on a weedy white gravel road. Follow the path downhill as it curves to the left. Because this area is relatively unwooded and sunny, the trailside brush sometimes grows so rapidly as to obscure the path. When in doubt, plow straight ahead. (If you look closely, you will see traces of fences, gateposts, and foundations indicating that this area was once a farmyard.) Follow the path to the right of a concrete-block shed.

Thirty-five yards beyond the shed fork right downhill. Continue straight downhill with a pine plantation on the left. At the bottom of the slope, follow the path as it curves left and climbs a small rise. Turn right on an obscure footpath sixty yards past the top of the rise. Continue downhill past a footpath intersecting from the left and another descending steeply from the right. Fork left to rejoin the main riverside path. Turn left downstream. With the river on your right, follow the path to Belair Road.

15

GUNPOWDER FALLS STATE PARK
Belair Road to Philadelphia Road
and Pulaski Highway

Walking — 5 or 7 miles (8 or 11.3 kilometers) depending on whether you cross the river at Philadelphia Road or at Pulaski Highway. Easy footpaths along both banks of the river. Between Philadelphia Road and Pulaski Highway the landscape changes from Piedmont to Coastal Plain. At high water there are frequent rapids along this stretch of river, which formerly was dammed at several points to power a succession of mills. Managed by the Maryland Park Service (592-2897).

THIS RIVERSIDE WALK passes the relics of some of the iron furnaces, forges, nail factories, and other industrial operations that were located along the Big Gunpowder Falls above and below the Philadelphia Road during the 18th and 19th centuries.

The early ironworks needed water power just like any other mill. Water power from low rock and wooden dams operated the bellows for the smelting furnaces and forges. Water also powered the mechanical hammers that beat the brittle pig iron to a

more malleable consistency after it had been reheated and refined in the forges. Other requisites were charcoal fuel made from cordwood, lime flux from limestone or oyster shells to coagulate impurities in the ore, and of course the ore itself.

Iron ore was found in many deposits near the western edge of the Coastal Plain. In fact, the presence of iron ore in the area around Baltimore had been recognized as early as 1608 when Captain John Smith, during his explorations of Chesapeake Bay on behalf of the Virginia Company, sent barrels of iron ore taken from the Patapsco River to England to be assayed. Smith even called the Patapsco *Bolus Flu* because of the nodules of ore that he found along its banks.

In 1719 Maryland's colonial legislature established a legal process to encourage the development of water power for the production of iron. The law stated in part: " . . .be it Enacted that if any person or persons shall desire to set up a forging mill or other convenience for carrying on Iron Works on land not before cultivated adjoining a stream, he may get a writ *ad quod dammum*" — that is, a writ of land condemnation. If the owner of the land refused to build a forge himself, the petitioner was granted a deed for one hundred acres, "the owner being paid for it." The law further provided: "If pig iron is not run in seven years, the grant is void." No fewer than twenty-three of these writs of private condemnation were granted between 1733 and 1767, most of which resulted in ironworks being built.

Blast furnaces of the period consisted of fat but hollow masonry stacks that were loaded through the opening at the top, which also served as the chimney. Once fired, the furnace was periodically recharged with alternating layers of ore, flux, and charcoal, and might be kept in blast for months at a time. Giant wood and leather bellows forced air in from the bottom. The higher of two taps was opened regularly to draw off the slag that floated on the molten iron. Then two or three times a day the lower tap was opened and the liquid iron was poured into molds. In the early years of this technology, the main pouring channel and the row of smaller grooves running to the molds were noted

I-95

Philadelphia Rd.

Pulaski Hwy.

Raphael Rd.

Mt. Vista Rd.

BIG GUNPOWDER FALLS

Forge Rd.

Belair Rd.

bus

parking

N

0   ¼   ½   ¾   1

mile

to resemble the outline of a sow with suckling pigs; hence the term "pig iron" for crude iron.

Considering the massiveness of the masonry furnaces, it is surprising how quickly they have been obliterated after their use ceased in the middle of the 19th century. Several of these structures were located along the stretch of the Big Gunpowder Falls called the Long Calm, where the Philadelphia Road used to ford the river. This area is about a quarter of a mile upstream from I-95. An early smelting furnace belonging to the Nottingham Company was located here, built in the 1750's. Nearby were Charles Ridgely's Long Calm Forges, erected at about the same time.

Because the owners of the Nottingham Company were either British or Loyalists, their property was expropriated during the Revolution by the state Office of Confiscated Effects. The Nottingham works were then sold at auction to the Ridgelys, who manufactured munitions for the Continental Army. The Ridgelys also made a variety of other products, as indicated by one of their newspaper advertisements:

> Cannon (from Nine to Two-Pounders), Bar-Iron, pig iron, pots from 15 gallons to three quarts, kettles from 45 to 15 gallons; Dutch-ovens, tea-kettles, skillets, salt-pans, flat irons, mortars and pestles, wagon-boxes, stoves, dripping pans and bakers... N.B. Castings of any sort made on the shortest notice.

After a period of disuse, the furnace and forges at the Long Calm were bought in 1845 by Robert Howard, principal of the Great Falls Iron Company, which had been chartered "for rebuilding and putting into operation the works heretofore known as Ridgely's Forges." Howard also operated a flour mill, saw mill, and large farm on the Big Gunpowder Falls. In 1846 he built a new furnace farther downstream which produced iron until about 1860. According to the 1850 census, Howard's Gunpowder ironworks had two furnaces and employed 120 hands. Output was 3,000 tons of pig iron produced from 7,500 tons of ore and 10,000 cords of firewood.

BUS: From downtown take the MTA Kingsville or Perry

Hall bus (both #15A) via Calvert Street, North Avenue, and Belair Road northeast out of the city. On weekdays you can ride all the way to the Gunpowder River. Tell the driver well in advance that you want to get off at the bridge. You will know that your stop is coming as the road descends into the wooded river valley after passing Perry Hall Road on the right. When you get off the bus, tell the driver to be expecting your return later in the day. For the return trip flag the bus from the wide gravel shoulder south of the bridge. On Saturday bus 15A goes only to Perry Hall, and you must walk 1.5 miles north on Belair Road to the river.

AUTOMOBILE: From the Beltway (I-695), Belair Road (Route 1) crosses Gunpowder Falls 5.4 miles northeast of Beltway Exit 32 North. A gravel parking area is located at the south end of the bridge on the downstream side. You will know that the bridge and pullout are coming when the road descends into the wooded river valley.

THE WALK: From the south end of the bridge and with the river on your left, follow the footpath downstream through the woods along the bank. Now and then the trail splits but soon rejoins. Continue on the riverside footpath downstream under the highway bridge at Route I-95.

Approximately two hundred feet upstream from the I-95 bridge, the path abruptly rises a few feet and passes above and to the right of the stone abutment of an old bridge. On the return trip, the matching abutment on the opposite bank is much more obvious.

About seventy-five yards below the I-95 bridge, large stones in the riverbed show bore holes two inches in diameter (visible, with some difficulty, at low water) indicating that a wooden dam was erected here and fastened to the rocks, which have since been pushed and tilted out of alignment. A millrace bolstered by a cut stone retaining wall (parts of which still stand) started at the south end of the dam. For a distance the path follows the filled-in mill race toward the site of Robert Howard's 1846 furnace, now a heap of rubble in back of a tavern on the Philadelphia Road. This furnace was thirty-one feet high. In 1856 it produced 1,100 tons of iron during thirty weeks of continuous blast.

Continue along the bank below the I-95 bridge toward the smaller bridge at Philadelphia Road (Route 7). Between these two bridges the path veers to the right away from the water up to a lawn by a tavern and oyster house. Follow the edge of the lawn to Philadelphia Road and then turn toward the bridge.

At this point you may return to Belair Road by crossing the bridge and following the riverside trail upstream along the north bank. For a longer walk, continue along the south bank to the bridge at Pulaski Highway (Route 40), and then go back upstream on the north bank to Philadelphia Road. In either case the footpath along the north bank is somewhat overgrown but still easily followed.

South of the present Philadelphia Road bridge (where another former ford was located), the asphalt path leads half a mile to a circular clearing that was the site of the Joppa Iron Works, also known as Patterson's Nail Mill. It was started in 1817 and continued in operation until 1860. In 1820 fifteen hands were employed producing sheet iron, barrel hoops, spikes, cut nails, and brads. By 1850 the Patterson Works employed 130 hands producing 36,000 kegs of nails per year. The following year the works was rebuilt to include six furnaces, one water-driven hammer, two trains of rolls to produce sheet iron, and thirty-seven nail machines to cut the nails from the sheets. The remains of a small brick heating furnace, now nothing more than a low brick rectangle full of weeds, are located sixty yards upstream from the Baltimore & Ohio Railroad bridge on the right-hand side of the path as you face downstream. On the opposite bank, a more substantial cut stone furnace is built into a cleft in the bedrock back a few dozen yards from the river's edge. At low

Low water, Big Gunpowder Falls

water the site of a former dam is marked by a row of twisted iron spikes sunk in the river bed just above the rapids. These rapids, incidentally, are the last on the Big Gunpowder and mark as well as any other point in the fall line zone the transition from the Piedmont to the Coastal Plain. If you continue downstream in order to return on the opposite bank after crossing the Route 40 bridge, notice the marked difference in landscape farther down the river.

As noted earlier, a former iron furnace is located on the north bank in a cleft in the rock near the last rapids on the river. The furnace is easy to miss, although as you approach it the quantity of slag in the path increases. After passing upstream under the railroad bridge, the path turns right uphill, then back to the left. In a few dozen yards, veer left past an intersection with a dirt road. Continue straight to a point of rock above the rapids. In doing so you will have walked directly across the top of the former furnace, which can be inspected by descending from the rock promontory on either side. To continue on the main path, return to the rock promontory, walk away from the river, and turn left on the first path upstream.

To return to Belair Road from Philadelphia Road, enter the woods on the riverside path starting at the end of the guard rail on the north bank. With the river on your left, follow the footpath upstream under the I-95 bridge and across a sloping concrete abutment. If necessary, sidestep across the abutment with your feet pointed toward the river to improve your balance and traction. Continue on the riverside footpath across several small streams and back to Belair Road.

16

FORT HOWARD

Walking — 1 mile (1.6 kilometers). The waterfront fortifications at the tip of North Point, with sweeping views east over the upper Chesapeake Bay, south across the mouth of the Patapsco River, and west to Sparrows Point. Freighters pass frequently and during winter ducks and geese gather in the coves. Telephone beforehand between noon and 4:00 P.M. on weekdays to make sure that the park has not been closed temporarily due to ongoing construction or seasonal budget constraints. Managed by the Baltimore County Department of Recreation and Parks (477-8330).

LIKE MAYAN RUINS overrun by jungle, several massive structures lie half-buried in the tangled brush and woods at the tip of North Point. All are of concrete empty, strangely abstract like the imaginary buildings in the drawings of M. C. Escher. These are the bunkers and huge amphitheater-like gun pits of Fort Howard, which during the first two decades of this century helped to guard the water approach to Baltimore.

Built at the end of the 19th century during the Spanish American War, Fort Howard never saw combat then, nor did it during World War I, when Forts Smallwood, Armistead, and Howard formed Baltimore's line of coastal defense against attacks that never came. The Fort Howard garrison, however, was said to maintain a high standard of proficiency. *The Baltimore Sun* for October 14, 1908, reported that the Howard gunners had been credited with setting a world's record for accuracy by hitting, nine times out of ten, a target that was being towed in the shipping channel nearly three miles away. The fort's guns included two batteries of twelve-inch mortars that fired projectiles weighing 1,000 pounds. The mortars were housed in the largest firing pits. Another emplacement held two twelve-inch disappearing rifles (i.e., modern rifled cannon — not smoothbore) that were raised for firing and lowered behind the revetment walls for loading. Four other emplacements (only three of which survive) housed six-inch, five-inch, and 4.7-inch rifles and three-inch rapid-fire guns.

In 1941, long after the guns had been removed, the fort was decommissioned as obsolete. The bunkers, barracks, officers' houses, and grounds were turned over to the Veterans Administration for development of the present hospital. Twenty-five years later the area occupied by the concrete revetments was returned to the Army for use by the intelligence school at Fort Holabird. During the Vietnam War, a mock Vietnamese village was constructed in the underbrush and vines among the old coastal batteries; here trainees were taught to interrogate prisoners of war.

When Fort Holabird was closed in 1972, its 62-acre parcel at North Point was deeded to Baltimore County by the General Services Administration under the federal government's Legacy of Parks program, by which surplus federal property is donated to local governments provided the land is used for recreation. Plans for the park's development include additional trails, a nature center, and facilities for camping, swimming, fishing, and picnicking. The hospital grounds, however, are not part of the park and are not open to visitors.

North Point is where four thousand English troops landed in the fall of 1814 for their abortive march on Baltimore. Major General Robert Ross, commander of the British army, had announced his intention to use Baltimore — that "nest of privateers" — as his headquarters during the coming winter. He

said that with the city as his base, his army would go where it pleased through Maryland.

Two years previously the youthful United States had declared war on England. In a petition to President Jefferson, Baltimore had even urged war with France as well on the grounds that her conduct was "scarcely less atrocious than that of England." Since 1793 England and France, at that time the world's two most powerful nations, had been locked in a protracted global war, and both countries regularly confiscated American merchant ships and cargoes in an attempt to prevent supplies from reaching the enemy. The United States itself engaged in the same practice during the Civil War, but in the early 1800's most Americans saw the seizures as a piratical violation of their neutral rights.

Ire toward England was intensified starting in 1805 by the British Navy's practice of stopping passenger vessels in United States coastal waters and removing all sailors whom the English surmised to be British subjects, for the Royal Navy was sorely in need of seamen. Also, the "war hawks," a group of congressmen from the frontier states, openly urged that war with Great Britain would enable the United States to seize Canada and its lucrative fur trade, to end the Indian menace in the Ohio Valley (where massacres and conspiracies were said to be incited by British agents), and to throw open more western land for settlement.

The war, however, did not go as planned. Successive attempts to invade Canada failed miserably. At Baltimore, the British blockade of Chesapeake Bay reduced the export trade to almost nothing. Among shipowners only the privateersmen made substantial profits through the seizure and sale of English merchant ships. Commissioned by the federal government as private warships, Baltimore's privateers captured about a third of all enemy vessels that were taken during the war. After being seized, the ships were sailed to American ports, where they and their cargoes were sold through judicial condemnation by admiralty courts.

In the spring of 1814, Great Britain and its allies finally

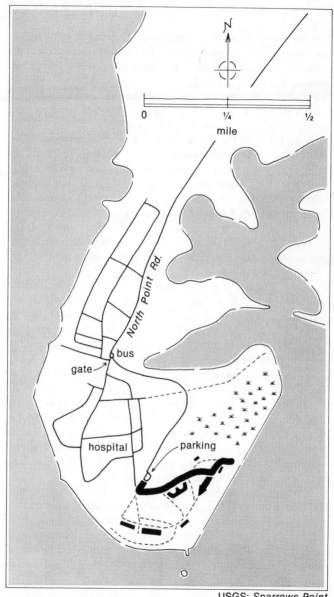

USGS: *Sparrows Point*

forced the abdication of Napoleon. England then turned its attention to the United States. The London newspapers announced that an expeditionary force of seasoned troops and sailors was being readied. "The seat of the American government, but more particularly Baltimore is to be the immediate object of attack .... Terms will be offered to the American government at the point of the bayonet."

In mid-August the British force appeared in Chesapeake Bay. Baltimore gained time while the English marched from the Patuxent River to Washington, which they captured on August 24, 1814. This event was enormously exaggerated in England, where the brief occupation of the national capital — a straggling, swampy place of 8,000 inhabitants — was touted by the British press to be equivalent to the fall of London. *The Times* of London declared, "The world is speedily to be delivered of the mischievous example of the existence of a government founded on democratic rebellion."

After only one day in Washington, where they burned the government buildings, the "modern Goths" — as one indignant American writer called the British — marched back to their ships. The armada sailed off down the Chesapeake, perhaps in an effort to lull Baltimore into thinking that the danger had passed, but they soon turned northward.

Meanwhile, Baltimore dug in. The previous year a half-million dollars had been raised by subscription among the residents for the defense of the city because no aid came from Washington. Fort McHenry had been strengthened and other shore batteries constructed. A line of earthworks over a mile long was thrown up to the east of the city at Hampstead Hill, across land now occupied by Patterson Park and Johns Hopkins Hospital. This was to be the main line of resistance.

Work on the fortifications continued until Sunday, September 11, when three alarm guns in the courthouse square and the ringing of bells announced the arrival of the British squadron of fifty ships at North Point, fourteen miles east of Baltimore at the mouth of the Patapsco River. After the militia had mustered, Major General Samuel Smith, to whom the city had assigned its defense, sent General John Stricker with 3,185 men out the Philadelphia Road to reconnoiter and to delay the enemy's advance. By that evening Stricker had reached the narrow neck of land between the head of Bear Creek and the Back River, about halfway between Baltimore and North Point. He deployed his men there, except for a contingent of cavalry and riflemen who were sent farther forward toward a farm owned by Robert Gorsuch.

At three o'clock the following morning, four thousand British soldiers rowed ashore in the dark at North Point. Their landing place at the tip of the peninsula was chosen because the Patapsco was thought to be too shallow for the larger ships to go farther upstream. The battle plan called for the smaller boats to push past Fort McHenry and to attack the city at the same time as the assault by land.

As light came on the British army advanced up North Point Road toward Baltimore. Eventually they stopped to rest while General Ross and his retinue left the road in order to get something to eat at the Gorsuch farm. According to Robert Gorsuch's grandson, the elder Gorsuch was forced not only to provide breakfast for the General and eight officers but also to eat and drink a sample of every dish that he served before the British would touch it. Talking of the coming battle while he ate, General Ross purportedly boasted that he would "eat his supper in Baltimore, or in hell."

Meanwhile, John Stricker (according to his account of the 12th of September) learned from his horse scouts that "the enemy in small force was enjoying itself at Gorsuch's farm." Two hundred and thirty infantry, some cavalry, and a cannon were immediately pushed forward. Stricker reported:

> This small volunteer corps had proceeded scarcely half a mile before the main body of the enemy showed itself, which was immediately attacked. The infantry and riflemen maintained a fire of some minutes and returned with some loss in killed and wounded; the cavalry and artillery, owing to the disadvantageous ground, not being able to support them.

The skirmish was more critical than the Americans thought. On the British side, an eyewitness account was provided by the Reverend Mr. Gleig, the military chaplain. He had been waiting with the main British force while General Ross breakfasted at the Gorsuch farm. After an hour the troops started to move again, but they had not traveled more than a mile when the "sharp fire of musketry was heard in front, and shortly afterward a mounted officer came galloping to the rear, who desired us to quicken our pace for that the advance guard was engaged." Gleig continued:

> At this intelligence the ranks closed, and the troops advanced at a brisk rate, and in profound silence. The firing still continued, though from its running and irregular sound, it promised little else than a skirmish; but whether it was kept up by detached parties alone, or by the outposts of a regular army, we could not tell because, from the quantity of wood with which the country abounded, and the total absence of all hills or eminences, it was impossible to discern what was going on at the distance of half a mile from the spot where we stood.

> We were already drawing near the scene of action, when another officer came at full speed toward us, with horror and dismay in his countenance, and calling loudly for a surgeon. Every man felt within himself that all was not right, though none was willing to believe the whispers of his own terror. But what at first we would not guess at, because we dreaded it so much, was soon realized; for the aide-de-camp had scarcely passed when the General's horse, without its rider, and with the saddle and housing stained with blood, came plunging onwards. In a few moments we reached the ground where the skirmishing had taken place, and beheld General Ross laid by the side of the road, under a canopy of blankets, and apparently in the agonies of death. As soon as the firing began he had ridden to the front, that he might ascertain from whence it originated and, mingling with the skirmishers, was shot in the side by a rifleman. The wound was mortal; he fell into the arms of his aide-de-camp, and lived only long enough to name his wife, and to commend his family to the protection of his country. He was removed towards the fleet, but expired before his bearers could reach the boat.

> It is impossible to conceive the effect which this melancholy spectacle produced throughout the army.... All eyes were turned upon him as we passed, and a sort of involuntary groan ran from rank to rank from the front to the rear of the column.

Nonetheless, the British pushed on until they ran into General Stricker's main force. A battle of an hour and a half followed. As the British troops advanced at a walking pace, the Americans fired what Gleig described as a "dreadful discharge of grape and canister shot, of old locks, pieces of broken muskets, and everything which they could cram into their guns." After firing one volley, part of the American line retreated without orders. As the lines of British approached nearer and nearer, firing as they came, General Stricker was forced to pull his troops back to the main line of fortifications outside the city.

The next day, after a bivouac at the North Point battlefield, the British slowly continued toward Baltimore, hindered by the trees which the retreating Americans had cut down across the road during the night. Rain fell all day and it was not until evening that the British covered the seven miles to Hampstead Hill, where they stopped in front of the American fortifications. Gleig reported:

> It now appeared that the corps which we had beaten yesterday was only a detachment, and not a large one, from the force collected for the defense of Baltimore.... Upon a ridge of hills which concealed the town itself from observation stood the grand army, consisting of twenty thousand men. Not trusting to his superiority in numbers, their general had there entrenched them in the most formidable manner, having covered the whole face of the heights with breastworks, thrown back his left so as to rest it upon a strong fort, erected for the protection of the river, and constructed a chain of field redoubts which covered his right and commanded the entire ascent. Along the line of the hill were likewise *fleches* and other projecting works, from which a cross fire might be kept up; and there were mounted throughout this commanding position no less than one hundred pieces of cannon.

The new British commander, Colonel Arthur Brooke, tried to

outflank the defenses by moving his troops to the north, but the Americans kept between the British and the city. Brooke then decided to try a night attack, provided he could receive support from the Navy. But, the English ships were repulsed at Fort McHenry, and Brooke eventually determined that attack was futile. In the early morning, while their ships continued the unsuccessful attack on Fort McHenry, the British began their retreat, which was not discovered by the Americans until daylight. The American troops were so worn out by the two days of watching and waiting, much of it in the rain, that General Smith decided not to counterattack. By the next day, the British had returned to their ships and were gone.

After the retreat the Baltimore newspapers dubbed the British the "night-retrograders." In England, however, *The Times* of London described the repulse at Baltimore and the contemporaneous naval defeat of the British at Plattsburg on Lake Champlain as a "lamentable event to the civilized world."

BUS: North Point is served by the MTA Fort Howard bus (#4) which for part of its route follows Dundalk Avenue south from Holabird Avenue. From downtown Dundalk Avenue can be reached by bus #10 or bus #20, from which you can transfer to bus #4 at the intersection of Holabird Avenue and Dundalk Avenue. Ride bus #4 all the way through Sparrows Point to the end of the line at the entrance to the Fort Howard Veterans Hospital. From the bus stop enter the park through the left gate. Follow the winding drive to the parking lot.

AUTOMOBILE: North Point and Fort Howard are reached via North Point Boulevard (Route 151) and North Point Road (Route 20). From Pulaski Highway (Route 40) turn southeast on Erdman Avenue, which then becomes North Point Boulevard. From the Beltway (I-695) take Exit 41 and follow Cove Road west to North Point Boulevard. Follow North Point Boulevard south, eventually forking left for North Point Road and Fort Howard. From the

entrance to Fort Howard Veterans Hospital, enter the park through the left gate and follow the winding drive to the parking lot.

THE WALK: From the far end of the parking lot, turn left on a wide asphalt path leading away from the fence and hospital lawn and into the woods. Fork left and continue to two huge concrete firing pits, each of which formerly held four twelve-inch mortars. This was Battery Key, named for Francis Scott Key.

Continue on the road past the rear of the mortar pits straight to another, smaller gun emplacement (Battery Clagett). Follow the path left of the revetments to the water's edge. To see a tidal pool and salt marsh formed behind the remains of the breakwater, follow the riprap for a short distance to the left.

Return to the small gun emplacement near the shore. Fork left past the rear of the revetments and follow the road parallel with the shore to the other batteries. The first to come into view is Battery Harris (five-inch guns), then Battery Stricker (twelve-inch guns on disappearing carriages), and finally Battery Nicholson (six-inch guns on disappearing carriages). At Stricker and Nicholson notice the hoists that lifted the shells and powder from the magazine to the gun platforms.

17

CYLBURN PARK

Walking — 1 or more miles (1.6 or more kilometers). The Victorian stone mansion, formal gardens, lawn, and woods of the old Tyson estate. Labels identify hundreds of varieties of trees, shrubs, flowers, and other plants. Over 150 species of birds have been seen here. Managed by the Baltimore City Department of Recreation and Parks (396-0180).

SUMPTUOUS CYLBURN PARK, Baltimore's horticultural center and arboretum, occupies 180 acres of meadow and woods on a high plateau above the Jones Falls Valley north of the Coldspring new town and south of Northern Parkway. A wide path follows the top of the bluff around three sides of the park and back across the meadow to Cylburn Mansion. The house now serves as headquarters for the Maryland Ornithological Society and the Cylburn Wildflower Preserve and Garden Center, Inc. Both organizations sponsor a variety of field trips, lectures, and other activities relating to natural history and gardening. For information on the programs and facilities of these two groups, write to them at Cylburn Park, 4915 Greenspring Avenue, Baltimore, Maryland 21209. The house itself is open from 7:30 until 3:30 on weekdays; the park from dawn until dusk every day. Picnicking and plant collecting are not permitted, and dogs must be leashed.

Started in 1863, Cylburn was developed during the decade following the Civil War as the country estate of Jesse Tyson, the son of Isaac Tyson, Jr., Baltimore's chrome king. The gray stone for the mansion was quarried at the Bare Hills west of Lake Roland, where the Tysons had some of their chromite and copper mines.

In 1888 Jesse Tyson married Edith Johns, a Baltimore debutante who in later years Alfred Jenkins Shriver listed in his will as among the ten most beautiful Baltimore women of his era (and all of whom, therefore, were by his testamentary directions painted together in a mural at Johns Hopkins University's Shriver Hall — each woman "at the height of her beauty"). The Tysons entertained frequently and lavishly at Cylburn, where they, their servants, and weekend guests arrived and departed by the Northern Central Railroad, which stopped at Tyson's private railway station just below Northern Parkway. Four years after Tyson's death in 1906, his widow married Lieutenant (later Major) Bruce Cotton, and for decades Cylburn continued to be a showplace where Baltimore society gathered for receptions in the large drawing room or wandered the lawns and gardens that were lit with hundreds of Japanese lanterns during summer musicales. Following Mrs. Cotton's death in 1942, Major Cotton sold the property to the city for a low price with the specific intention that the estate be made a city park.

If you want to learn to identify trees, the large variety of labeled specimens at Cylburn Park provides excellent practice and an enjoyable excursion at all times of year. Oak, hickory, and tulip trees (also called yellow poplar) and to a lesser extent maple, beech, and ash dominate the scene, as is typical in eastern Maryland. Dogwood, sassafras, and mountain laurel are also widespread in the understory.

Although many of these trees and shrubs are tolerant of a wide range of soil and moisture conditions, some prefer a particular type of terrain where they flourish and even supplant other species. For example, swamp white oak generally grows in

moist or even soggy soils, as one would suppose from its name. Willow oak and pin oak are most often found in heavy bottom-land soils. Most oaks, however, including white, scarlet, black, chestnut, and chinquapin oak, are found in drier soils. Southern oak usually grows in poor upland regions. And blackjack oak and post oak have a particularly high tolerance for dry, gravelly hilltops, where with the evergreen eastern red cedar, pitch pine, and Virginia pine they become the dominant species.

Similarly, each type of terrain is associated with certain groups of trees. Stream banks support river birch, elm, syca-more, witch hazel, red and silver maple, box elder, and black, green, and pumpkin ash. The lower slopes of hills, valleys, and ravines sustain beech, sweetgum, tulip trees, black tupelo, dogwood, and mountain laurel. And, on upper slopes and ridge-tops the balance shifts toward the dry oaks, white ash, and shagbark and pignut hickory.

Learning to identify trees is easy. Every walk or automobile trip is an opportunity for practice. Notice the overall forms and branching habits of the trees, and also the distinctive qualities of their twigs, buds, bark, leaves, flowers, and fruits or seeds. These are the key identification features that distinguish one species from another. Finally, when using a field guide, check the maps or descriptions that delineate the geographic range within which the tree or shrub is likely to be found.

Some trees, of course, have very distinctive and reliable forms. Familiar evergreens like balsam fir and eastern red cedar have a conical shape, like a dunce cap, although in dense stands the red cedar tapers very little and assumes the columnar form of the Italian cypress, which it somewhat resembles in other ways as well. The deciduous little-leaf linden, imported from Europe and used as a street tree, is more or less conical. Elm displays a spreading form like a head of broccoli. A full-bodied egg shape is characteristic of sugar maples and beeches, although both will develop long branchless trunks in crowded woods, as do most forest trees competing for light. The vertically exaggerated cigar shape of Lombardy poplars — a form called fastigiate — and the pendulous, trailing quality of weeping willows are

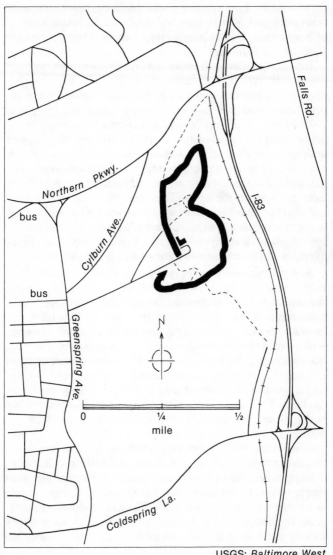

USGS: *Baltimore West*

unmistakable. For ornamental use, fastigiate varieties of some other trees have been isolated and cultivated, including varieties of Norway maple and Chinese ginkgo, the later being a common street tree in Baltimore.

Branching habit is an important clue to some trees, and one observable even at a distance. White pine, for example, has markedly horizontal branches with a slight upward tilt at the tips, like a hand palm upward. Norway spruce, usually seen as an ornamental tree dwarfing and darkening a house near which it was planted fifty or a hundred years ago, is a very tall evergreen with long, evenly spaced, drooping lower branches. The slender lower branches of pin oak slant downward, while those of white oak and red oak are often massive and horizontal, especially on trees growing in the open. The lower branches of the horse chestnut (another European import) also droop but then curl up at the tips in chunky twigs. Elm branches spread up and out like the mouth of a trumpet. And, the trunk of the honey locust diverges into large branches somewhat in the manner of an elm.

A good botanist or nurseryman can identify trees by their twigs alone, — that is, by the end portion of the branch that constitutes the newest growth. During winter the shape, color, size, position, and sheathing of the buds are important. For instance, beech buds are long and pointed, tan and sheathed with overlapping scales like shingles. Sycamore and magnolia buds are wrapped in a single scale. The twigs of horse chestnut are tipped with a big, sticky, brown bud, while those of silver maple and to a lesser extent red maple end with large clusters of red buds. Some oaks, such as white oak, have hairless terminal buds, while other species, such as black oak, have hairy end buds.

Aside from buds, other characteristics of twigs are color, thorns, hair, pith, and the size, shape, and position of leaf scars marking where the leaf stems were attached. For example, most maple twigs are reddish brown, but the twigs of striped maple and mountain maple are greenish. Thorns and spines are significant because relatively few trees have them, notably honey locust, black locust, Hercules club, prickly ash, buckthorn bumelia, Osage orange, American plum, some crab apples, and the many varieties of hawthorn. Most oaks have hairless twigs, although some species such as blackjack oak are distinctly hairy. As for pith, it can be chambered, solid, spongy, or different colors depending on the species. It was noted earlier that oak, hickory, and tulip trees are common forest species near Baltimore, yet of the three only the twigs of tulip trees have chambered pith, while the pith of white oak in cross-section forms a star. Finally, in winter the location of leaf scars in opposite pairs along the twigs (as with maples) distinguishes a wide variety of trees and shrubs from those with leaf scars arranged alternately, first on one side then the other (as with oaks). All of these distinguishing features can best be appreciated simply by examining the twigs of different species.

Bark is not always a reliable clue, since its color and texture often change with age or differ between trunk, branches, and twigs. Often the distinctive character of bark is only seen in the trunks of large, mature trees. Bark can be smooth, furrowed, scaly, plated, shaggy, fibrous, criss-crossed, corky, or papery. Some trees, of course, are unmistakable because of their bark. The names shagbark hickory and paper birch (a northern species not found in Maryland) speak for themselves. Striped maple has longitudinal, whitish stripes in the smooth green bark of the younger trees. The criss-crossed ridges of white ash, the light blotches on sycamores, and the smooth gray skin of beech are equally distinctive. Other peculiarities of bark are also helpful. For example, birches and some cherries are characterized by horizontal lenticels like random dashes.

Everybody notices leaves. Most obvious is the overall shape. Gray birch (seen in Maryland as an ornamental tree) is triangular, catalpa heart-shaped, sweetgum star-shaped, beech elliptical (or actually pointed at each end), and black willow narrower still and thus "lanceolate." Notice also the leaf margin or edge. Is it smooth like rhododendron, wavy like magnolia, serrated like basswood, or deeply lobed like most maples? And how many lobes are there? Tulip trees, for example, have easily recognized four-lobed leaves, maples three or five. Also, are the lobe tips rounded like white oak or pointed like red oak? Or, as with sassafras and red mulberry, does the same tree have differently shaped leaves, the most distinctive being those with a single asymmetrical lobe creating a leaf outline like a mitten.

Some leaves such as Japanese maple, horse chestnut, and buckeye are palmately compound, meaning that they are actually composed of leaflets radiating from the end of the stem like fingers from the palm. In the fall the whole compound leaf drops off the tree as a unit. Other leaves, such as ash, hickory, and sumac, are pinnately compound, being composed of leaflets arranged in pairs along a central stalk. Still other leaves are *bi*-pinnately compound, somewhat like a fern. The leaflets grow from stalks which in turn spread from a cental stalk. Honey locust, Kentucky coffee tree, and the ornamental imported silk tree are examples.

Although the needles of evergreens are not as varied as the leaves of deciduous plants, there are still several major points to look for. One is the number of needles grouped together. White pine has fascicles of five; pitch pine, loblolly pine, and sometimes shortleaf pine have fascicles of three; and red pine, Virginia pine, Austrian pine, and sometimes shortleaf pine have fascicles of two. Needles of spruce, hemlock, and fir grow singly, but are joined to the twig in distinctive ways. Spruce needles grow from little woody pegs, hemlock needles from smaller bumps, and fir needles directly from the twig, leaving a rounded pit when pulled off. Spruce needles tend to be four-sided, hemlock flat, and fir somewhere in between. Larch needles (which drop off in winter) grow in dense clusters.

Flowers are a spectacular though shortlived feature of some trees and shrubs. Three variables are color, form, and (less reliably) time of bloom. Redbud, with red-purple clusters, and shadbush (also called Allegheny serviceberry), with small, white, five-petalled flowers, are among the first of our native Eastern trees to bloom, perhaps as early as late March in Maryland. In April comes dogwood. The blossoms of flowering dogwood consist of four white, petal-like bracts, each with a brown notch at the tip, while the flowers of alternate-leaf dog-

Black Oak, Quercus velutina

wood (also common in Maryland) consist of loose white clusters. Mountain laurel and rhododendron bloom in late spring and early summer. These are a few of our native species commonly thought of as flowering trees and shrubs, but the blossoms of other species are equally distinctive; for instance, the small but numerous flowers of maples appear in some species in advance of the leaves. The tulip-like flowers and durable husks of tulip trees are also unusual in appearance. Unlike most trees, the yellow flowers of witch hazel appear in fall or winter.

Finally, the seeds or fruit of a tree are a conspicuous element in summer and fall, sometimes lasting into winter and even spring. Nobody who sees a tree with acorns could fail to know that it is an oak, although some varieties, such as willow oak, are otherwise deceptive. Distinctive nuts are also produced by beech trees, horse chestnuts, hickories, and walnuts. Some seeds, like ash and maple, have wings. Others, such as honey locust, Kentucky coffee tree and redbud, come in pods like beans and in fact are members of the same general legume family. The seeds of birches, poplars, and willows hang in tassels, while those of sweetgum and sycamore form prickleballs (as do the shells of horse chestnut and buckeye). And, of course, brightly colored berries and fruits are produced by many species, such as holly, hawthorn, and hackberry. Among needle evergreens, spruce and pine cones hang from the twigs, while fir cones stand upright, and the small hemlock cones grow from the twig tips.

BUS: From downtown take the MTA Belvedere and Greenspring bus (#19) via Eutaw and North avenues and Garrison Boulevard to the intersection of Greenspring and Cylburn avenues. You will know that your stop is coming when the bus passes Sinai Hospital and turns uphill from Belvedere Avenue onto Greenspring Avenue. The MTA Sinai Hospital bus (#1) also runs to Greenspring and Cylburn avenues. And, MTA bus #44 passes the intersection of Belvedere and Greenspring avenues a short distance north of the entrance to the park.

CYLBURN PARK

AUTOMOBILE: *The entrance to Cylburn Park is marked by stone posts on the east side of Greenspring Avenue 0.3 mile south of Northern Parkway and 0.7 mile north of Coldspring Lane. The address is 4915 Greenspring Avenue.*

THE WALK: *Start your walk from the circular drive in front of Cylburn Mansion, where you can pick up maps and brochures. Follow the asphalt drive to the left of the house and past the herb garden on your right. Continue straight into the woods on the broad footpath to the left of the carriage house. Pass the first trail leading to the right. Continue gradually downhill for two or three hundred yards before turning right on a narrow footpath that is marked by several wooden steps. This path is what the map available at the mansion calls the Azalea Trail. (The broad trail that you are leaving leads downhill to the railroad tracks under the overpass at Northern Parkway where the Tysons used to have their private railroad station.)*

Follow the Azalea Trail around the hillside, at one point turning sharply right where another footpath leads downhill to the left. The path eventually reaches a large trail intersection near the lawn and formal garden. If you want to extend your walk, turn left back into the woods and follow the Circle Trail clockwise around the rim of the bluff. But be sure to visit the formal gardens and other displays in back of the mansion before you leave.

18

GWYNNS FALLS PARK

Walking — 3 miles (4.8 kilometers). A winding path that follows the level course of a former mill race along the side of Gwynns Falls Valley, with views out over the stream and bottomland to the opposing hillsides. Good birdwatching. Managed by the Baltimore City Department of Recreation and Parks (396-0010).

GWYNNS FALLS PARK is the eastern, older half of Baltimore's largest park complex. The other half is Leakin Park. Totaling about 1,200 acres, these two adjacent parks include the steep valleys of Gwynns Falls and its tributary Dead Run at the western edge of the city. Together they are Baltimore's principal "wilderness" reservation, so that it is here possible to take a walk in a forest of immense oak, hickory, ash, sycamore, beech, and tulip trees entirely within the city limits.

Gwynns Falls is named for Richard Gwynn, who in 1669 (more than fifty years before Baltimore was founded) obtained a monopoly on commerce with the Indians and established a fortified trading post on the stream west of present-day Carroll Park. In time the river powered a series of mills, including, as of 1795, three flour mills of the Ellicott family near Frederick Avenue. Other mills were established farther upstream, notably

the Powhatan woolen mills near Woodlawn, the Ashland mills at present-day Dickeyville, and a grist mill at Franklintown, where a small cluster of stone buildings still stands on Franklintown Road just beyond the western boundary of Leakin Park.

In 1893 the Olmstead Brothers, Boston's pre-eminent land planning firm and consultants to many eastern cities, presented their *Report upon the Development of Public Grounds for Greater Baltimore*. The Olmstead report recommended that the city develop a comprehensive park system based on stream valleys and adjacent lands, as has since been done at Gwynns Falls, Herring Run, Stony Run, and to a lesser extent at other streams within the city. Gradually Gwynns Falls Park and Leakin Park have been pieced together by a series of purchases between 1902 and 1969, when the 100-acre Windsor estate on Windsor Mill and Wetheredsville roads was acquired.

For decades now the big parks at Gwynns Falls and Dead Run have been the focus of public debate. For a period in the early 1970's, squalls of litigation emanated from the surrounding highlands in an inconclusive effort to block the use of the parks as an expressway route for Interstate-70 from Frederick. This freeway has long been scheduled to be the final link in Baltimore's legendary 3-A highway system. More recently, however, an abiding fog seems to have settled over the valleys as other highway projects have consumed all available funds.

Baltimore's highway saga started in the early 1940's, when freeway planning for the city first raised the possibility of a crosstown expressway to replace Route 40, at that time a major interstate road. In the 1950's and early '60's the Harbor Tunnel Thruway and most of the Beltway were built, carrying interstate traffic around the city while yet providing highway access to Baltimore's port area and industrial southeastern sector. Planning and more planning continued, however, for an east-west expressway *somewhere* through the middle of Baltimore.

In 1962 a city-wide hearing was held at Eastern High School on the recommended alignment for the entire inner-city highway system, consisting of I-70, I-95, and I-83. When the discussion turned to the segment of I-70 through Gwynns Falls

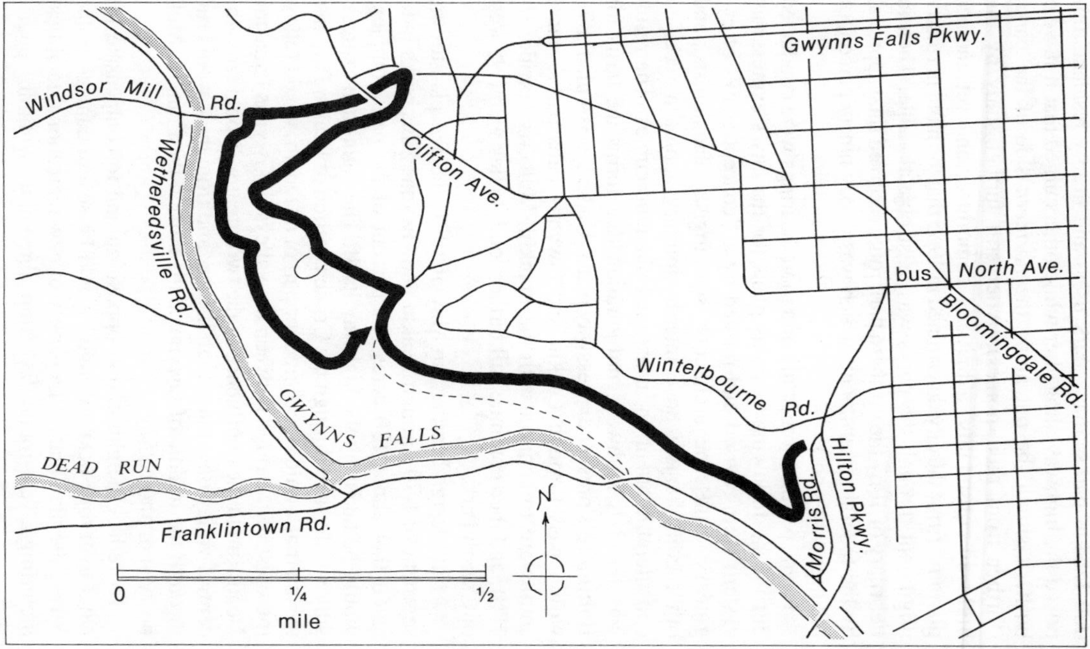

USGS: *Baltimore West*

and Leakin parks, many park users and nearby residents opposed the highway altogether while others urged that if it were built, it should be put along the *northern* side of the parks (farther from their homes). After still further study by the highway consultants, a mayoral committee, and yet another planning firm, the city determined in 1965 that the more northerly alignment through the parks was least objectionable. Then in February of 1967 the northern park route received final approval by the federal government, which was to pay ninety percent of the highway's cost.

Even so, still more study and more hearings were conducted during the following years as plans for the city's expressway system were revised and refined by a "concept team" of engineers, landscape architects, sociologists, economists, and other consultants whose interdisciplinary approach received considerable attention in national planning circles. The result was the 3-A highway configuration that forms the basis for Baltimore's present expressway plans. Under the 3-A plan, I-70 would pass through Leakin and Gwynns Falls parks, curve southward to connect with the Franklin-Mulberry corridor (I-170), and then continue still farther south to link with I-95 west of Carroll Park.

At a "design hearing" in May of 1971, the 3-A plan for the segment of I-70 through Leakin and Gwynns Falls parks indicated that about 130 acres (11 percent of the park complex) would be taken by the highway itself. The eight-lane expressway would slice through the Crimea section of Leakin Park in a trench that would be covered for part of its length, would follow the crest of the ridge between the valleys of Gwynns Falls and Dead Run to the confluence of the two streams, would cross the central valley on a long, high bridge, and from there would run through the middle of Gwynns Falls Park to the Franklin-Mulberry spur and I-95.

To reduce neighborhood opposition and to compensate for what everyone acknowledged would be severe damage to the parks, the plan featured a variety of new recreational facilities, including a year-round day camp, three new swimming pools, more than thirty tennis courts, and several new ballfields at intervals around the rim of the valleys, as well as an extensively refurbished trail system and the clearing or thinning of three hundred acres. The planners' report said that this program of recreational development would restore the remaining parkland to the functional equivalent of a park without a highway, but many opponents saw the proposal simply as a further degradation of the unique wilderness character of the park. Other neighborhood groups who had little use for the passive character of the park liked the recreational improvements but for the most part still opposed the highway. Meanwhile, implementation of the plan for added recreational facilities was made a major condition for federal financing of the highway under §4(f) of the Department of Transportation Act of 1966, which requires "all possible planning to minimize harm" to public parks.

In 1971 the highway controversy flared into litigation. Opponents of the park route filed a series of suits against city, state, and federal officials to bar acquisition of the right-of-way and to prevent construction. In the first suit Tom Ward, a lawyer and former city councilman, alleged that because the city had purchased Leakin Park with the proceeds of a gift restricted to park use, the conversion of parkland for a highway would be a breach of trust. This claim was rejected by the Maryland Court of Appeals, although the Court ruled that any compensation received by the city for relinquishing part of Leakin Park would have to be used to expand or improve the remaining park.

Ward brought yet another suit in federal district court. It was consolidated for trial with a companion case filed against Secretary of Transportation John Volpe and other officials by the Sierra Club and a corporation calling itself Volunteers Opposing Leakin Park Expressway (V.O.L.P.E., Inc.). The Sierra Club's complaint alleged every conceivable flaw in the highway planning process, but the court focused on the limited issue of whether the various public hearings concerning the placement of I-70 through Leakin and Gwynns Falls parks satisfied federal requirements. Stating that a major purpose of a "location hearing" is to present for public comment alternative alignments for the highway, the court noted that at the 1962 hearing only the one route — the southern route — had been proposed through Leakin Park. This route later had been rejected in favor of the northern park alignment, which the court said never had been presented with or without alternatives at a hearing intended to elicit comments on the highway's location. In consequence, federal approval was voided and another location hearing was required to be held, as was done in December, 1972, six months after the court's decision.

At the new hearing so many people wanted to speak that the meeting had to be continued for three additional evenings. Representatives of local business organizations favored the park highway, as they always had. Area residents, however, were nearly unanimous in their opposition to all eight alternative routes that were presented, although some speakers urged that the park be developed for active recreation. Following the hearing, city and state agencies again approved the northern park route.

In yet a *third* highway suit decided in 1973, the park plaintiffs joined another anti-expressway coalition (M.A.D., Inc., standing for Movement Against Destruction) to stop work on the Franklin-Mulberry spur until an environmental impact statement under the National Environmental Policy Act of 1969 had been prepared for the entire 3-A highway system. Because the western end of the Franklin-Mulberry highway is planned to join I-70, the park plaintiffs feared that the vast expense of the Franklin-Mulberry project (more than $100 million as of 1980) would become justification for construction of the park highway as well, even though the environmental effects of I-70 had not been evaluated when the Franklin-Mulberry spur was approved. The court ruled, however, that the Franklin-Mulberry highway was not so interrelated to the other expressway segments that the whole system needed to be evaluated together.

After the spate of litigation in the early 1970's planning for the park segment of I-70 continued for a period, but then slowed and in most respects stopped. In a tentative agreement reached in 1974, the Federal Highway Administration undertook to pay for the proposed recreational development of the parks as an integral part of highway construction, if the Secretary of Transportation again were to approve the project. A revised and expanded environmental impact statement — prepared in draft form for the 1972 hearing — was completed in 1975 but then never released. Nor was the project again submitted for federal review, so low was its priority compared to other segments of the 3-A system. Now so much time has passed that new hearings, an updated environmental statement, and comparative studies of different transportation systems would be required prior to again seeking federal approval which, if it were given, would probably trigger another round of litigation.

In other developments, spokesmen for Baltimore's business community, which for years urged that the park highway was needed as a link in the truck route between the port and the Midwest, have begun to say that I-95 and the Beltway provide adequate access to I-70 west of the city, and that the central business district might be better served by other transit projects. Planners say that if the highway is built, it will be primarily a commuter artery for the western suburbs, but they also note that runaway gasoline prices are steadily increasing the attractiveness of some alternative transportation systems.

Most significantly, highway costs are outstripping revenues. At 1979 prices (projecting eight percent inflation through 1985 and no inflation after that) the planners estimate that the completion of the 3-A system would cost about $2 billion. To finish I-70 alone would require $500 million, plus another $100 million for the link to the Franklin-Mulberry corridor. These costs are almost certainly going to increase faster than projected — just as they already have. During the late 1970's the composite index for the cost of highway construction increased 18 percent per year, which translates into a doubling of cost every four years. Although the federal government pays ninety percent (and that practice may end), the local ten percent is still substantially more than William K. Hellman, the third chief of the Interstate Division for Baltimore City to wrestle with the 3-A system, estimates that the city will receive as its share of state automobile registration fees, gasoline taxes, and other highway revenues during the 1980's.

Finally, as the existing system of local streets, bridges, and expressways has aged, a larger proportion of funds has been required for maintenance. In 1981 Baltimore's Major William Donald Schaefer proposed paying for the repair of various city-owned bridges by using federal funds earmarked for the park segment of I-70. And, other projects such as the construction of railroad overpasses to prepare for the advent of mile-long coal trains are assuming added urgency. Thus, if I-70 continues to occupy last place on the city's list of street and transportation projects, that is tantamount to never building the highway at all.

BUS: This walk starts near the west end of North Avenue. Coming from the east, take the MTA Walbrook bus (#13) via North Avenue; from downtown take the MTA Belvedere and Greenspring bus or Walbrook Jct. bus (both #19) via Eutaw and North Avenue. In either case get off at the intersection of North Avenue and Hilton Parkway. You will know that your stop is coming when the bus climbs past Poplar Grove, Longwood, and Rosedale streets.

From the corner of North Avenue and Hilton Parkway, walk south (or downhill) on Hilton Parkway a quarter of a mile to Morris Road on the right.

AUTOMOBILE: The walk starts at the intersection of Hilton Parkway and Morris Road, a quarter of a mile south of the intersection of Hilton Parkway and North Avenue. Park on one of the nearby residential streets east of Hilton Parkway and above the intersection with Morris Road.

THE WALK: From the intersection of Hilton Parkway and Morris Road, follow Morris Road downhill but fork right in fifty yards onto a broad dirt path sloping gradually uphill. Follow the path uphill and then around to the right away from Hilton Parkway. Continue on the wide path as it winds along the side of the Gwynns Falls Valley. At an

intersection with a disused asphalt road, turn right and follow the old asphalt road uphill. Immediately beyond a barrier across the road, turn sharply left uphill on another road leading past low stone walls and through a meadow. Pass a road leading left at the crest of the hill, then fork right immediately onto a crumbling asphalt road leading downhill into the woods. Follow the path through the woods as it gradually curves right. Continue to the Clifton Avenue Bridge.

Cross Clifton Avenue and follow Monticello Road downhill to Windsor Mill Road. Turn left on Windsor Mill Road and follow it downhill under the bridge. About 100 yards in front of a bridge over Gwynns Falls, turn left into the woods on a wide dirt path. Follow the path along the flank of the bluff to the four-way intersection with the unused asphalt road that you previously followed uphill. Cross the asphalt road and follow the dirt path along the edge of the bluff back to your starting point.

19

LEAKIN PARK

Walking and ski touring — 3 miles (4.8 kilometers). The broad lawns, hillside trails, woods, and mansion at Crimea, an imposing private estate that has been preserved as a city park. A livery for riding horses is planned. Managed by the Baltimore City Department of Recreation and Parks (396-0010).

THIS WALK EXPLORES CRIMEA, the country estate developed with a trainload of rubles by Baltimore's rolling-stock magnate, Thomas DeKay Winans. The massive, almost cubic stone mansion was built shortly before the Civil War to overlook the valley of Dead Run at the western edge of the city. Named for the Soviet Riviera, Crimea was Winans's dacha — his summer home and winter hunting lodge. His intown residence was Alexandroffsky, formerly located in a private walled park east of present-day Union Square and described in various accounts as "palatial," "magnificent," "exotic," and "fabulous." Two cast-iron lions that used to guard Alexandroffsky were removed when it was razed in 1927 and now stand near the lion cages at the zoo in Druid Hill Park. Crimea fared better than Alexandroffsky and is now a part of Leakin Park, where several miles of bridle paths follow the wooded slopes.

The story of Winans's Russianisms and his Russian millions starts with his father, Ross Winans, a prominent inventor in the early days of the Baltimore & Ohio Railroad. After traveling abroad with a commission sent by the B&O to study the English railroad system in 1828, Ross Winans worked on the adaptation of English engines and rolling stock to the steep grades and tight curves of the new American railroads. He reduced the friction of railroad wheels by fusing them with axles so that the entire assembly revolved as a unit, with the axle turning in grease-packed boxes. This arrangement, with some modifications, is still in use around the world. Winans put the flange of the wheels on the inside edge and invented the swivel wheel truck and coned wheels with beveled treads to help trains negotiate curves. He was the first to use horizontal pistons on his *"Crab"* locomotives, and in time he built increasingly powerful engines, such as the *Camel* and the *Mud Digger,* to pull the B&O over the Allegheny Mountains. In 1835 Ross Winans and a partner assumed management of the B&O locomotive and rolling-stock shops at Mt. Clare under an arrangment allowing them to sell equipment to other lines, provided that the B&O had first call. Then, in 1844 Ross Winans left the B&O and set up his own shop, where he built the *Carroll of Carrollton,* a locomotive so fast for its day that its potential speed could never be tested because the railbeds were not sufficiently straight or evenly graded for the engine to be fully opened.

All of which brings us to the Russians, who in the late 1830's were embarking on their own railroad program. Czar Nicholas I had ordered the construction of a line between St. Petersburg and Moscow. Two Russian engineers came to the United States in 1839 to study American railroads and rolling stock, and they eventually recommended to the Russian government that George W. Whistler, a civil engineer trained at West Point (and incidentally father of the artist James A. McNeill Whistler), be hired to superintend construction of the new Russian line. Major Whistler knew Ross Winans; he and Winans had served together on the B&O commission to England, and Whistler had helped survey the B&O route. Whistler also thought highly of Winans's

locomotives and abilities. At Whistler's suggestion, Ross Winans was offered a contract in 1842 to set up a shop in Russia to manufacture rolling stock in partnership with the Philadelphia firm of Harrison and Eastwick, which had been recommended by the two Russian engineers. Ross Winans declined on the grounds that he was too old, but he persuaded Whistler and the Russians to accept his two sons, Thomas and William, both of whom had worked under Ross in positions of responsibility.

In 1844 Harrison and Eastwick closed their Philadelphia locomotive shop and shipped their equipment to Alexandroffsky near St. Petersburg, where they were joined by the Winans brothers. A new shop was established and the partners embarked on an immensely lucrative contract to supply two hundred locomotives and seven thousand cars for the new Russian railroad, dubbed "the harnessed samovar" by the local populace. In 1850 the contract was expanded to include more equipment and ongoing maintenance. William Winans also designed and built iron bridges for the railroad, which was being laid out by Major Whistler. The Americans are said to have entertained lavishly, and judging from the estates that the Winans later built here and in England, they became accustomed to life in the grand style.

Thomas Winans returned home in 1854, three years after completion of the railroad. He brought with him a Russian wife of Italian and French ancestry. William Winans stayed in Europe and never returned to the United States. Nor did Major Whistler, who had encountered constant difficulties and delays in the construction of the railbed. Weakened by cholera, he died in 1849 before the line was completed.

Following his return to Baltimore, Thomas Winans designed and had constructed at his father's shop a streamlined "cigar ship." It was completely cylindrical and tapered to a point at each end like a submarine but was limited to surface travel. This design was intended to increase speed and economy by minimizing water resistance and top-heaviness in high winds and seas. Four of Ross Winans's locomotive engines powered a turbine-like wheel that completely circled the ship's waist,

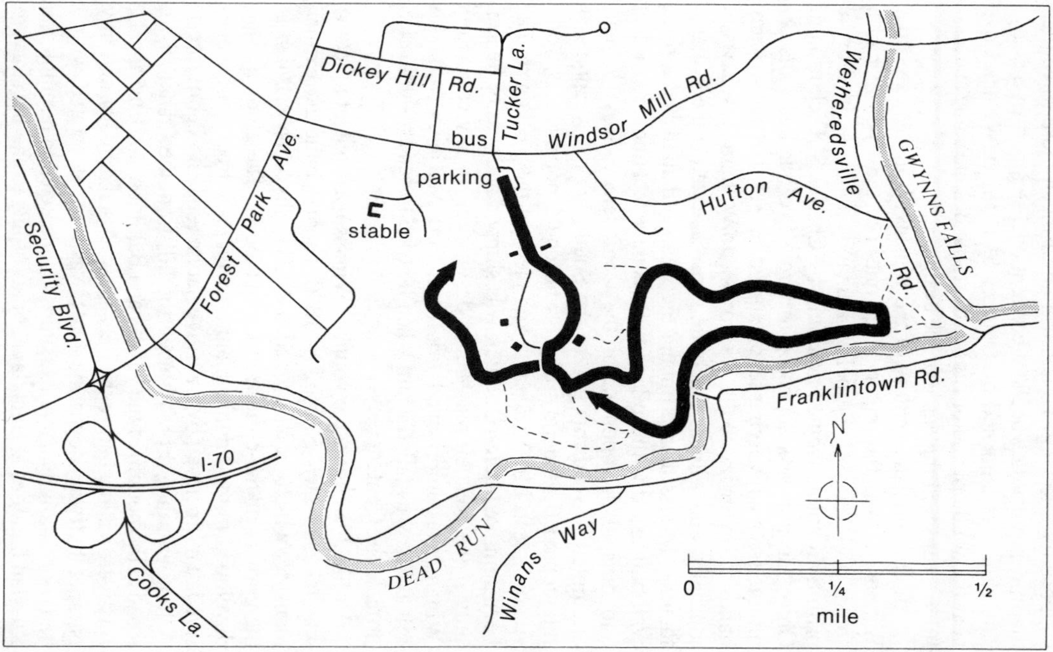

GWYNNS FALLS

Wetheredsville Rd.

Hutton Ave.

Franklintown Rd.

Windsor Mill Rd.

Tucker La.

bus

parking

Dickey Hill Rd.

stable

Forest Park Ave.

Winans Way

DEAD RUN

I-70

Cooks La.

Security Blvd.

N

mile

0   ¼   ½

USGS: Baltimore West

supposedly allowing the application of much more force than the midship paddlewheels of conventional steamers of the day. The ship was launched on October 6, 1858, at Winans Cove near the southern end of Light Street, but despite some successful test runs nothing came of the design.

Another unusual venture of the Winans — in this case Ross Winans — was the repair at the outset of the Civil War of a steam-powered, self-propelled armored cannon — in short, a primitive tank. Invented and built by Charles S. Dickinson of Ohio, the gun was supposed to throw two hundred balls per minute from a revolving set of cupped arms, "just like so many hands throwing baseballs," according to William H. Weaver, a journalist and witness when the gun was tested at the Winans' factory. In less than a minute the weapon demolished a brick wall buttressed with a pile of timbers three feet thick. An ardent and outspoken supporter of the Confederacy, Ross Winans attempted to send this gun to the South, but the weapon was intercepted by federal troops, who could not make it work. According to Mr. Weaver, a key piece of the mechanism had been removed before the gun was shipped and was to be sent only if the weapon reached its destination. In any case, Ross Winans was imprisoned briefly at Fort McHenry; after his release he was jailed again when he tried to send a shipload of arms to the Confederacy.

Unlike his father, the younger Winans was content to let the war take its own course. In 1860 Thomas built the Crimea mansion, which shows a touch of Russia in its ornate carvings at the corners of the cornice and porch posts. The grounds were developed in the English manner, with large trees amid extensive lawns enclosed by a curving naturalesque border of forest. A long entrance drive climbed the hill from the Franklintown Road at the bottom of the valley, and Baltimore and Chesapeake Bay were visible before the trees grew. A semicircular masonry parapet halfway down the bluff was once decorated with a battery of dummy cannons, supposedly erected to resemble the Russian batteries at Balaklava, or according to another story, to deter passing Union troops from molesting the estate. A large

Cinnamon Fern, Osmunda cinnamomea

undershot waterwheel that is still located near the Franklintown Road pumped spring water to the house, and a gasworks manufactured gas for the principal residence. Near the main dwelling is the "Honeymoon House," which Winans built for his daughter when she married. The estate also has a caretaker's house, a wooden "American Gothic" chapel, a large stone stable, and a vegetable cellar and ice house set into the slope at the bottom of the valley. The ground floor of the main house now serves as park headquarters; the second floor is the residence of one of the park staff.

In 1866 Thomas Winans returned to Russia, where he served as president of the firm of Winans, Whistler, and Winans, managers of the St. Petersburg and Moscow Railroad under an eight-year contract with the Russian government. The Whistler in the firm's name was the son of the former superintendent and also the Winans' brother-in-law, having married Julia Winans while working in Ross Winans's Baltimore shops. After the management contract had run only two years, however, the Russian government took over the work and released the firm with the payment of a settlement of several million dollars. Thomas Winans returned home and divided his time among his houses, travels, and various charities until his death in 1878.

In 1941 part of the Crimea estate was purchased for a city park from Thomas Winans's heirs, and eight years later the city bought the balance. In both instances the purchase money was provided from the bequest of J. Wilson Leakin, an attorney who had died in 1922. Leakin had left several downtown properties to the city with the stipulation that the proceeds from their rental and eventual sale be used for the acquisition and improvement of a new city park. For fifteen years different neighborhood groups and municipal agenicies wrangled about where the park should be located. Even after the first Crimea tract was purchased, Mayor Thomas D'Alesandro favored selling the property in 1947 because he thought it inaccessible, but he later changed his mind after visiting the park and instead recommended that it be expanded.

LEAKIN PARK

BUS: From downtown the MTA Security Square/West-view/Lorraine Park bus (#15) passes the Crimea entrance to Leakin Park at the intersection of Windsor Mill Road and Tucker Lane. You will know that your stop is coming when the bus turns off Forest Park Avenue onto Dickey Hill Road and then turns uphill onto Tucker Lane. From the bus stop, cross Windsor Mill Road and enter the park between the two stone posts surmounted by cast-iron eagles.

AUTOMOBILE: The Crimea entrance to Leakin Park is on Windsor Mill Road directly opposite the intersection with Tucker Lane about a quarter of a mile east of the corner of Windsor Mill Road and Forest Park Avenue. Enter the park between the stone posts surmounted by cast-iron eagles and park in the lot on the left of the entrance drive.

THE WALK: Follow the entrance drive past the tennis courts, a wooden chapel, and a caretaker's house. Fork left and follow the entrance drive to the Crimea mansion.

    About a hundred yards after passing the front of the mansion, turn left off the driveway onto a dirt road and then left again at a "T" intersection. Follow the path downhill, but turn left at the first opportunity along a swale leading downhill across the lawn below the mansion. Re-enter the woods and continue downhill to a semicircular parapet about twenty yards in diameter, where Thomas Winans's dummy cannons used to be mounted.

    Turn left and follow the trail slightly uphill along the slope, past two trails leading left, and downhill across a small masonry bridge with iron hoop railings. Continue along the flank of the valley and then gradually downhill past immense tulip trees. Eventually turn right at a "T" intersection and then right again at the edge of Dead Run.

    With Dead Run on the left, follow the trail upstream, across some bottomland, and past a low stone wall to a large clearing. Follow the left edge of the lawn past a bridge and gradually uphill as the lawn curves right and narrows. Turn left where the trail that you followed earlier crosses the lawn in a grassy swale below the mansion. Follow the dirt road uphill past the road intersecting from the right. Continue straight through the woods past another trail intersection and then downhill to the right. The trail eventually emerges at a broad lawn, with the entrance drive visible in the distance.

20

HERRING RUN

Walking — 3 miles (4.8 kilometers). A wasteland of weeds, marsh, low brush, woods, and rubbish along both banks of Herring Run, currently awaiting park development. What could you do if you were in charge? Managed by the Baltimore City Department of Recreation and Parks (396-8256).

ALTHOUGH SHOWN ON THE CITY's master plan as potential park, the banks of Herring Run between Sinclair Lane and Pulaski Highway are as yet largely undeveloped for park purposes, nor are there any proposals for improvement of the area in the near future. Most of the west bank is weedy meadows and willow thickets crisscrossed by trail bike paths. The mounded east bank is recent landfill. Herring Run itself, which carries stormwater runoff from the northeast sector of the city and from parts of Baltimore County, is a sort of urban arroyo of gravel bars and gabions — that is, crushed rock encased in large wire cages along the banks to retard erosion. Nonetheless, as Lancelot Brown, the 18th-century English landscape architect, would have said, this unprepossessing wasteland "has capabilities" — a phrase Brown used so often that he became known as Capability Brown.

Now it is your turn to exercise your capacity for park design. If you have taken some of the other walks in this book, you have had a chance to form your own opinions about what makes a successful park. You undoubtedly have seen (and occasionally have smelled and heard) some of the problems of gross misuse, under- and overuse, and conflicting use from which parks suffer. This walk has been included here despite its crudeness so that you can examine a stretch of land that is currently in limbo and determine what you would recommend, were you the city's planning consultant.

Upstream from Sinclair Lane, Herring Run already has been developed into Baltimore's longest linear park, stretching from Baltimore County south past Mount Pleasant Golf Course, Morgan State, and Lake Montebello. So, if you are repelled by the section of Herring Run explored by this walk, you can recover your spirits by following the winding asphalt path along either bank of the stream between Harford and Belair roads.

In Baltimore the impetus to create or refurbish a park usually comes from nearby neighborhoods. Herring Run is somewhat unusual because planning for the whole stream valley and its tributaries, from Hillendale and Chinquapin Run in the north to Back River in the south, is coordinated by the Herring Run Public Watershed Association and its Commission. Composed of representatives from Baltimore County, Baltimore City, and the state, the Commission tends to concentrate on matters of health and safety requiring regional cooperation, such as water pollution and flood control.

Matters of more local interest are for the most part left to the large Herring Run Citizens Advisory Committee, composed of representatives of improvement associations from neighborhoods bordering the stream. The Advisory Committee meets yearly to discuss a lengthy agenda of specific neighborhood concerns, such as local playgrounds and illegal dumping. If this group expresses a persistent interest in the area south of Sinclair Lane, it is likely that the city will eventually arrange for the preparation of a park development plan to explore the issue.

Obviously, one of the first steps taken by the park planner is

inspection of the area to determine the basic terrain with which he must work, as well as those less permanent features of the landscape that are worth preserving and enhancing. In recent years standard land planning practice has included a site inventory and analysis of such factors as topography, slopes, geology, soils, stream patterns and quality, vegetation and forest types, animal life, historic sites, and existing facilities, although it is sometimes difficult to determine afterwards what practical use has been made of the information. The planner must also note problems that need to be remedied, such as eyesores that should be screened with trees and shrubs. And, access must be provided from major roads and surrounding residential areas as well as between separate areas of the park.

Soil (or more accurately rubbish) is a critical factor at Herring Run. Much of the land along the stream between Sinclair Lane and Pulaski Highway is underlaid by unburned refuse that will continue to settle for many years. The futility of building playing fields on this foundation of trash is demonstrated by just such an attempt in 1978 near Armistead Gardens on the west bank by the Harbor Tunnel Thruway, where large hollows have developed in the fields since they were graded in 1978.

After becoming familiar with the area, the planner then meets with the residents of nearby neighborhoods to determine their general concerns and recommendations as well as their long shopping list of specific requests for different kinds of facilities, from tennis courts to tot lots. Despite his preconceptions about what might be suitable, the planner quickly learns that most residents want facilities that will provide conveniences and amenities for their own use or that will improve the tone of the neighborhood but attract as few outsiders as possible. Residents bordering the park understandably expect that facilities that attract crowds — even something as innocuous as a bicycle path — be located deep within the park at a distance from their homes. In most instances a consensus gradually is reached through a series of public meetings, where objections and proposed solutions are reviewed.

In addition to site characteristics and neighborhood prefer-

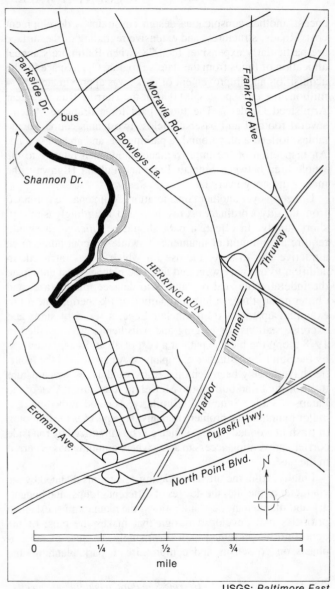

USGS: *Baltimore East*

ences, another conspicuous design constraint is development cost. Roads, structures, and extensive regrading of the surface are particularly expensive. In 1978, when Baltimore's annual allocation of funds from the state's Program Open Space for the acquisition and improvement of parks was approximately $1.4 million, the city spent $500,000 in the Herring Run area near Armistead Gardens. The funds paid for a drainage system, several football and baseball fields, two tennis courts, picnic tables, toilets, a playground, a parking lot, and an access road. An inspection of the improvements shows that relative to the whole area between Sinclair Lane and Pulaski Highway, the money did not go very far.

Upkeep is yet another consideration. Maintenance is funded from the city's ordinary tax revenues and accordingly is in very short supply. In effect, a park should be *efficient:* it should require a minimum of maintenance while yet continuing to be attractive and to serve the use for which it was intended. In addition to ordinary wear and tear, the planner must anticipate the indefatigable zeal of vandals to deface, smash, raze, and obliterate anything of less than Gibraltar-like permanence. For example, upstream from Sinclair Lane, a series of signs and exercise stations for jogging and calisthenics was installed in 1978 along the bicycle path at a cost of about $4,000 (donated by the Sun Life Insurance Company of America), but the facilities have largely been demolished by vandals, as was a nature trail for the blind built at the McKeldin Recreation Area of the Patapsco Valley State Park. Similarly, as noted at the outset, a major maintenance problem in many large parks is the dumping of trash in wooded places, which can be minimized by roadside barriers preventing access to areas where dumping has occurred in the past.

Finally, from the often conflicting constraints dictated by the character of the site, the desires of different groups, and budgetary and maintenance considerations, the planner must establish priorities and develop a design that makes the most of the opportunities presented. Not surprisingly, because of the emphasis on consensus and compromise in park planning, the

Herring Run Park, a multiple-use facility

result is sometimes a discouraging blandness that is exemplified by the stretch of Herring Run immediately north of Sinclair Lane. Any ideas for the area to the south?

BUS: From downtown take the MTA Cedonia bus (#5) via Baltimore, Gay, Preston, and Federal streets to Herring Run. Get off at Shannon Drive or Parkside Way, where Sinclair Lane crosses Herring Run. You will know that your stop is coming when the bus turns right from Clareway onto Sinclair Lane.

AUTOMOBILE: The portion of Herring Run Park that is the focus of this walk stretches southeast from the Sinclair Lane bridge along both banks of Herring Run. The bridge is located 0.8 mile east of the intersection of Sinclair Lane and Erdman Avenue.

THE WALK: From the Sinclair Lane bridge follow the west bank of Herring Run downstream with the river on your left. If brush along the river blocks your way, follow the asphalt path and then the dirt road that runs farther back from the water's edge. Where a small stream joins Herring Run from the right (or west), follow the dirt path along the precipitous bank to a lawn and bridge and then back to Herring Run on the opposite bank.

To examine the east bank of Herring Run, return to Sinclair Lane and then walk downstream as you did on the west bank.

BIBLIOGRAPHY

Numbers in the parentheses at the end of the citations refer to the chapters in this book that are based on the cited material.

Abbott, Collamer L. "Isaac Tyson, Jr., Pioneer Mining Engineer and Metallurgist," *Maryland Historical Magazine,* March, 1965. (6)

The Allen Organization. *Study for a Proposed Gunpowder River Valley Park System.* Maryland State Planning Commission, 1958. (8)

Allen, Paul. *Conservation Easements.* Baltimore, Maryland Environmental Trust, 1977. (7)

Andrews, Matthew Page. *History of Maryland: Province and State.* Garden City, New York, Doubleday, Doran & Company, 1929. (16)

Andrews, Matthew Page. *Tercentenary History of Maryland.* Chicago, S.T. Clarke Publishing Company, 1925. (16)

Baltimore Region Water Quality Management Plan — Summary: Clean Enough for Fishing and Swimming? Baltimore, Regional Planning Council, 1979. (12)

Baylin, Lee. "Md. Still Seeking to Buy Park Lands 13 Years Later," *The Evening Sun,* July 22, 1971. (8)

Bee, Avery M. "Wool-Weaving Dickeys Have A 100-Year Record," *The Sun,* March 27, 1938. (3)

Borror, Donald J. *Common Bird Songs.* New York, Dover Publications, Inc., 1967. (10)

Brockman, C. Frank. *Trees of North America.* New York, Golden Press, 1968. (17)

Carson, Larry. "State Moving To Buy Houses In Park," *The*

Evening Sun, March 31, 1978. (8)

"City To Purchase Rest Of Leakin Park Tract," *The Evening Sun,* April 8, 1947. (19)

Collins, Joan. "Daniels — History of a Lost River Valley," *Ellicott City Heritage,* September, 1979. (4)

Corbett, Edward S. "Water Resources in the Urban Forest Environment," In *Proceedings of the National Urban Forestry Conference, Washington, D.C., November, 1978; ESF Publication 80-003, 1980. (12)*

Corbett, Edward S. and Warren Spencer. "Effects of Management Practices on Water Quality and Quantity; Baltimore, Maryland, Municipal Watersheds," In Municipal Watershed Management Symposium Proceedings, USDA Forest Service General Technical Report NE-13. (12)

"Crimea Picked Finally for Leakin Park," *The Sun,* June 8, 1940. (19)

Daniel, Mann, Johnson & Mendenhall. *Master Development Plan: Patapsco State Park.* Annapolis, Maryland Department of Forests and Parks, 1971. (5)

"A Day at the Crimea," *The Sunday Herald,* April 22, 1894. (19)

"Dickey Mill Now Industrial Park," *The News American,* September 16, 1973. (3)

Dilts, James D. "Can State Clean Up Polluted Patapsco?" *The Sun,* August 20, 1967. (5)

Dilts, James D. "Death Of A Town," *The Sun,* May 12, 1968. (4)

Dunn, Linda. "Old Mill Houses Of Daniels To Come Tumbling Down," *The Sun,* May 23, 1967. (4)

Gilbert, Kelly. "City eyes giving bridges to state," *The Evening Sun,* March 23, 1981. (18)

Hugh Ely v. David Steward and J.J. Speed, Trustees, 2 Md. 408 (1852). (4)

The Elysville Manufacturing Company v. The Okisko Company, 5 Md. 152 (1853). (4)

The Elysville Manufacturing Company v. The Okisko Company et al., 1 Md. ch. 392 (1849). (4)

BIBLIOGRAPHY

Evans, Charles W., ed. *Biographical and Historical Accounts of the Fox, Ellicott, and Evans Families*. Buffalo, Baker, Jones & Co., 1882. (1, 3, 4)

Final Environmental Statement. Report No. FHWA-MD-EIS-72-10-D-F. U.S. Department of Transportation, Federal Highway Administration; Maryland Department of Transportation, State Highway Administration, 1975. (18)

"Ft. Howard Opens Park Doors," *The Dundalk Times*, September 18, 1975. (16)

"Fort Howard water plan set," *The Sun*, April 20, 1977. (16)

Garrels, Robert M. *A Textbook of Geology*. New York, Harper & Brothers, 1951. (13, 14)

Gottschalk, L.C. *Report on the Reconnaissance Sedimentation Surveys of Loch Raven and Prettyboy Reservoirs, Baltimore, Maryland*. Washington, D.C., United States Department of Agriculture, Soil Conservation Service, 1943. (8)

Greene, Suzanne Ellery. *An Illustrated History: Baltimore*. Woodland Hills, California, Windsor Publications, Inc., 1980. (6)

Gunpowder Falls State Park: Concept Plan. Annapolis, Department of Natural Resources, 1978. (8)

Hartley, Brent A. "Current Management Practices on the Baltimore Municipal Watersheds," In *Municipal Watershed Management Symposium Proceedings*, USDA Forest Service General Technical Report NE-13, 1975. (11, 12)

Hartley, Brent A. and Warren G. Spencer. "Management Problems and Techniques on a City Watershed," paper presented at National Urban Forestry Conference, Washington, D.C., November, 1978. (11, 12)

Hay, Jacob. "Crimea, The Mansion Rubles Built, Opens Doors To All Of Baltimore," *The Sun*, June 14, 1948. (19)

Henry, Frank. "City Playground — 37 Miles Long," *The Sun*, November 5, 1950. (5)

Henry, Frank. "Patapsco State Park — Maryland's Second Biggest Park," *The Sun Magazine*, August 14, 1956. (5)

Hines, Bob. *Ducks at a Distance*. Ottawa, Canadian Wildlife Service, 1965. (10)

Holland, Celia M. *Ellicott City, Maryland: Mill Town, U.S.A.* Chicago, Adams Press, 1970. (3)

"Home Of Mrs. Bruce Cotten, Cylburn Will Be Public Park," *The Sun*, September 29, 1942. (17)

Hughes, T. Lee. "V.O.L.P.E. a Road Block," *The News American*, August 22, 1971. (18)

"Jackson Calls Group To Act On Leakin Bequest," *The Evening Sun*, July 1, 1938. (19)

James, Alfred R. "Sidelights on the Founding of the Baltimore & Ohio Railroad," *Maryland Historical Magazine*, December, 1953. (3)

Joynes, J. William. "Company Town," *The News American*, December 9, 1956. (4)

Keene, John C. *Untaxing Open Space*. Washington, D.C., Council on Environmental Quality, 1970. (7)

Klein, Richard D. *An Integrated Watershed Management Policy for Baltimore County, Maryland*, Annapolis, Maryland Department of Natural Resources, 1980. (12)

Kreh, Charles F. "Saw Ellicott City Flood And Tells Grim Story of Awful Havoc There," *The Sun*, February 15, 1920. (1)

Levin, Alexandra Lee. "A Russian Railroad Made The Winans Family Rich," *The Sun Magazine*, October 10, 1976. (19)

Marye, William B. "A Commentary on Certain Words and Expressions Used in Maryland," *Maryland Historical Magazine*, June, 1951. (9)

Mayre, William B. "Place Names of Baltimore and Harford Counties," *Maryland Historical Magazine*, September, 1958. (15)

Maryland Geological Survey: Baltimore County. Baltimore, Johns Hopkins Press, 1929. (6, 13, 14)

McKerrow, Stephen. "Daniels Mill Is Declared A National Historic Site," *The Evening Sun*, May 14, 1973. (4)

McGrain, John W. *Grist Mills in Baltimore County, Maryland*. Towson, Maryland, Baltimore County Heritage Publication, 1980. (2, 3)

McGrain, John W. "Historical Aspects of Lake Roland," *Maryland Historical Magazine*, September, 1979. (10, 12)

BIBLIOGRAPHY

McGrain, John W. *The Molinography of Maryland: A Tabulation of Mills, Furnaces, and Primitive Industries*. Towson, Maryland, 1968. Revised and expanded, 1976. (1, 2, 3, 4, 10, 15)

Morison, Samuel Eliot. *The Oxford History of the American People*. New York, Oxford University Press, 1965. (16)

Movement Against Destruction v. Volpe, 361 F. Supp. 1360 (D. Md. 1973). (18)

Nielsen, Craig A. "Preservation of Maryland Farmland: A Current Assessment," *University of Baltimore Law Review*, Vol. 8, No. 3, 1979. (7)

Northern Baltimore County Citizens Committee. *Hereford Area Plan: Gunpowder State Park*. 1979. (8)

"Over $1,800,000 Flood Damage in Park; River Changes Course; Public Warned About Danger," *The Catonsville Times*, July 20, 1972. (1)

Overview Statement for Interstate 70N and Interstate 170 in West Baltimore, Baltimore, Maryland. U.S. Department of Transportation, Federal Highway Administration; Maryland Department of Transportation, State Highway Administration, 1975. (18)

"Park Expansion Imperils 4 Homes," *The News American*, February 28, 1979. (8)

"Park Section Is Dedicated," *The Sun*, June 17, 1957. (5)

"Patapsco Courses 50 Miles From Pond To Port," *The Evening Sun*, November 2, 1976. (5)

Patapsco Valley State Park: Concept Plan. Annapolis, Department of Natural Resources. 1976. (5)

Patapsco Valley State Park: Draft Master Plan. Annapolis, Department of Natural Resources. 1977. (5)

"Patapsco's Beauty To Be Preserved," *The News American*, June 6, 1912. (5)

Pearre, Nancy C. and Allen V. Heyl. *Chromite and Other Mineral Deposits in Serpentine Rocks of the Piedmont Upland, Maryland, Pennsylvania and Delaware*. Geological Survey Bulletin 1082-K. Washington, D.C., Government Printing Office, 1960. (6)

211

Peterson, Roger Tory. *How to Know the Birds*. New York, Mentor Books, 1949. (10)

Petrides, George A. *A Field Guide to Trees and Shrubs*. Boston, Houghton Mifflin Company, 1958. (17)

Phieffer, C. Boyd. "Soldiers Delight," *The News American,* March 17, 1968. (6)

Phillips, Thomas L. "Orange Grove as a Busy Mill Village," *The Sun Magazine,* June 25, 1967. (2)

Phillips, Thomas L. *The Orange Grove Story*. Washington, D.C., 1972. (2)

Platt, Rutherford. *American Trees, A Book of Discovery*. New York, Dodd, Mead, & Company, 1952. (17)

Porter, Eliot. *Birds of North America*. New York, E.P. Dutton Co., Inc., 1972. (10)

Program Open Space — Ten Year Report: 1969-1979. Annapolis, Department of Natural Resources, 1980.

Report of the Mayor's Advisory Committee on Herring Run to the Mayor and City Council of Baltimore City. 1977-1978. (20)

Robbins, Chandler S., Bertel Bruun, and Herbert S. Zim. *Birds of North America*. New York, Golden Press, 1966. (10)

Robbins, Chandler S. and Danny Bystrak. *Field List of the Birds of Maryland*. Maryland Ornithological Society, 1977. (10)

Robbins, Michael W. *Maryland's Iron Industry During the Revolutionary War Era*. Annapolis, Maryland Bicentennial Committee, 1973. (15)

Scarupa, Henry. "A Ghost Town With A Band," *The Sun Magazine,* October 14, 1973. (15)

Scharf, Thomas J. *The Chronicles of Baltimore*. Baltimore, Turnbull Brothers, 1874. (16)

"$180,000 Set For Leakin Park Use," *The Evening Sun,* March 27, 1947. (19)

"Shrinking Maryland Farmland," *The Sun,* February 15, 1981. (7)

Siegel, Eric. "Saving Open Land," *The Sun Magazine,* July 6, 1980. (7)

Stump, William. "The Man Behind The Iron Horse," *The Sun Magazine,* February 24, 1952. (19)

BIBLIOGRAPHY

Stump, William. "Street Signs: Cylburn Avenue," *The Sun Magazine*, July 18, 1954. (17)

Tuemmler, Fred W., and Associates. *Master Development Plan: Gunpowder River Valley State Park*. College Park, Maryland, 1967. (8)

Urban Design Concept Associates. *Corridor Development: Baltimore Interstate Highway System 3-A/Segment 9*. 1970. (18)

Vokes, Harold E. and Jonathan Edwards. *Maryland Geological Survey*. Baltimore, 1974. (6, 13, 14)

Walsh, Jean. "This Week Marks A Century Since The Great Flood," *The Catonsville Times*, July 25, 1968. (1)

Walsh, Richard and William Lloyd Fox, eds. *Maryland, A History: 1632-1974*. Baltimore, Maryland Historical Society, 1974. (3, 16)

Ward v. Ackroyd, 344 F. Supp. 1202 (D. Md. 1972). (18)

Ward v. Mayor and City Council of Baltimore, 267 Md. 576, 298 A.2d 382 (1973). (18)

Warfield, J.D. *The Founders of Anne Arundel and Howard Counties, Maryland*. Baltimore, Kohn & Pollock, 1905. (3)

Joseph White and Thomas White v. The Okisko Company, et al., 3 Md. ch. 214 (1852). (4)

Whyte, William H. *The Last Landscape*. Garden City, New York, Doubleday & Company, Inc., 1968. (7)

"Will The East-West Highway Ever Get Built," *The News American*, April 8, 1974. (18)

"Winans Steam Gun Mystery Is Solved," *The News American*, April 12, 1911. (19)

"The Winans Steamer," *Harper's Weekly*, October 23, 1858. (19)

ABOUT THE AMC

The Appalachian Mountain Club is a non-profit volunteer organization of over 25,000 members. Centered in the northeastern United States with headquarters in Boston, its membership is worldwide. The AMC was founded in 1876, making it the oldest and largest organization of its kind in America. Its existence has been committed to conserving, developing, and managing dispersed outdoor recreational opportunities for the public in the Northeast and its efforts in the past have endowed it with a significant public trust and its volunteers and staff today maintain that tradition.

Ten regional chapters from Maine to Pennsylvania, some sixty committees, and hundreds of volunteers supported by a dedicated professional staff join in administering the Club's wide-ranging programs. Besides volunteer organized and led expeditions, these include research, backcountry management, trail and shelter construction and maintenance, conservation, and outdoor education. The Club operates a unique system of eight alpine huts in the White Mountains, a base camp and public information center at Pinkham Notch, New Hampshire, a new public service facility in the Catskill Mountains of New York, five full service camps, four self-service camps, and nine campgrounds, all open to the public. Its Boston headquarters houses not only a public information center but also the largest mountaineering library and research facility in the U.S. The Club also conducts leadership workshops, mountain search and rescue, and a youth opportunity program for disadvantaged urban young people. The AMC publishes guidebooks, maps, and America's oldest mountaineering journal *Appalachia*.

We invite you to join and share in the benefits of membership. Membership brings a subscription to the monthly bulletin *Appalachia;* discounts on publications and at the huts and camps managed by the Club; notices of trips and programs; and, association with chapters and their meetings and activities. Most important, membership offers the opportunity to support and share in the major public service efforts of the Club.

Membership is open to the general public upon completion of an application form and payment of an initiation fee and annual dues. Information on membership as well as the names and addresses of the secretaries of local chapters may be obtained by writing to: The Appalachian Mountain Club, 5 Joy Street, Boston Massachusetts 02108, or calling during business hours 617-523-0636.